Recovery from Eating Disorders

Recovery from Eating Disorders

A Guide for Clinicians and Their Clients

Greta Noordenbos

WILEY-BLACKWELL

A John Wiley & Sons, Ltd., Publication

This edition first published 2013
© 2013 John Wiley & Sons, Ltd

Wiley-Blackwell is an imprint of John Wiley & Sons, formed by the merger of Wiley's global Scientific, Technical and Medical business with Blackwell Publishing.

Registered Office
John Wiley & Sons, Ltd, The Atrium, Southern Gate, Chichester, West Sussex, PO19 8SQ, UK

Editorial Offices
350 Main Street, Malden, MA 02148-5020, USA
9600 Garsington Road, Oxford, OX4 2DQ, UK
The Atrium, Southern Gate, Chichester, West Sussex, PO19 8SQ, UK

For details of our global editorial offices, for customer services, and for information about how to apply for permission to reuse the copyright material in this book please see our website at www.wiley.com/wiley-blackwell.

The right of Greta Noordenbos to be identified as the author of this work has been asserted in accordance with the UK Copyright, Designs and Patents Act 1988.

Library of Congress Cataloging-in-Publication Data
Noordenbos, Greta.
  Recovery from eating disorders : a guide for clinicians and their
clients / Greta Noordenbos.
     pages   cm
  Includes bibliographical references and index.
  ISBN 978-1-118-46920-0 (cloth) – ISBN 978-1-118-46919-4 (pbk.)
1. Eating disorders–Risk factors.   2. Eating disorders–Treatment.   I. Title.
  RC552.E18N64 2013
  616.85′2606–dc23

                                        2012036588
A catalogue record for this book is available from the British Library.

Cover image: Diana Ong, *Abstract #10*, 1965. Private collection. © Diana Ong/SuperStock.
Cover design by Nicki Averill Design & Illustration.

Set in 10/12pt Sabon by SPi Publisher Services, Pondicherry, India
Printed in Malaysia by Ho Printing (M) Sdn Bhd

1   2013

Contents

About the Author

Dr. Greta Noordenbos is a senior researcher in the Department of Clinical Psychology, Leiden University, the Netherlands. She completed her doctoral thesis on cultural and gender factors in the development of anorexia nervosa in 1987. She then conducted research on several topics in the field of eating disorders: risk factors and prevention, long-lasting and chronic patients, criteria for recovery, quality of treatment, emotion regulation and alexithymia, inner criticism and self-esteem. In 1994, she founded the Dutch Committee for Prevention of Eating Disorders and participated in the Specialized Interest Group for Prevention of the Academy of Eating Disorders. She has written several books and articles on eating disorders. Together with Professor Walter Vandereycken from Leuven University in Belgium, she edited the Dutch version of the *Handbook of Eating Disorders*. She was also a member of the Task Group of the Dutch Guidelines for Eating Disorders and became an honorary member of the Dutch Academy of Eating Disorders in 2010.

Address for correspondence:
Dr. Greta Noordenbos: Department of Clinical Psychology,
Leiden University. Wassenaarseweg 52
2333 AK, Leiden, The Netherlands.
Noordenbos@FSW.Leidenuniv.nl

Foreword

This book describes in a unique way the conditions necessary to recover from an eating disorder. Greta Noordenbos is one of the few experts in this field who has done research into these aspects. This book reflects the knowledge and insights she developed about the recovery process of eating disorder patients. What makes this book unique is that she writes from the perspective of the patients and the way they think and feel. The stories of many such patients are given in detail here. The author makes very clear how important it is to listen to eating disorder patients carefully and with respect, and try to understand what is going on in their minds.

The information provided in this book will be very useful not only for patients, but also for their families and the therapists involved in the process of recovery from the eating disorder. It becomes clear that recovery is much more than ensuring enough food intake, weight recovery and reducing binging and purging. Although they are necessary conditions for recovery, it is also important that eating disorder patients gain insight into their own feelings, needs and wishes and learn to express their emotions. They also have to improve their body image and develop more self-esteem and empower their identity. Moreover, they have to improve emotion regulation and social relationships. Many quotations from former patients illustrate which factors helped them to recover. This book will certainly motivate eating disorder patients to ask for help and so take the first steps towards recovery. For that reason, I would advise every patient, parent and therapist to read this book.

Dr. Johan Vanderlinden
Psychologist-psychotherapist
University Psychiatric Centre of Catholic University in Leuven,
Psychological Faculty of Leuven University,
Belgium

Acknowledgements

I would first like to thank all the eating disorder patients I interviewed. This book could not have been written without their inputs about their process of recovery. They inspired me to write this book, because they are the best guides to inform clinicians, professionals, parents and friends what it means to develop an eating disorder and to recover from it. They have shown that full recovery is indeed possible. Recovered patients are also important role models for all those who continue to suffer from eating disorders.

The first edition of this book, entitled *Gids voor herstel van Eetstoornissen*, was published in 2007 in the Netherlands by De Tijdstroom, Utrecht. Many readers stimulated me to publish an English version of this book. I would like to thank Joanna Kortink, Liesbeth Libbers, Carmen Netten, Ellen Spanjers, Johan Vanderlinden and many other professionals for their support and De Tijdstroom for their permission to publish an English version of this book.

The English version, entitled *Recovery from Eating Disorders: A Guide for Clinicians and Their Clients*, has been completely rewritten and updated with new assignments and questionnaires. I am very grateful for all the useful comments of my international colleagues to improve this book: Tabita Björk, Runi Börreson and Rachel Bryant-Waugh. Darren Reed was very helpful in getting this book published. Many thanks also to Ineke Smit who carefully corrected my English. Without their support and valuable suggestions, I would never have been able to publish this book.

Greta Noordenbos
Leiden University,
The Netherlands

Introduction

Can eating disorder patients recover? What changes should they make in order to recover? For a long time, the most important goals for recovery were normalizing their eating habits and weight. Although these goals are necessary steps in the process of recovery, they are not enough. Eating disorder patients struggle not only with food and weight, but also with very negative thoughts about their bodies and themselves. They are often very critical about themselves, and if they are not able to cope with their own high standards, they think they have failed and blame themselves. They also have problems with emotion regulation and social relationships. In order to recover from their eating disorder, they have to change many aspects of their lives: not only their eating habits and weight, but also their self-evaluation and body attitude, their feelings and emotions, and their relations with others.

To find out what changes are necessary for eating disorder patients in order to regain full health, I interviewed nearly a hundred former female and male patients about their process of recovery. They talked about the difficult period before their eating disorder and the first stage of their dieting regime, which was often felt as a *solution* to their problems. The positive feelings in this first stage of the eating disorder encouraged them to continue their dieting behaviour. However, the longer they continued dieting, the more severe were the negative physical, psychological and social consequences, which made their lives very difficult and lonely. Confronted with all these negative consequences, they slowly realized that they had to change their eating habits in order to recover.

Recovery from Eating Disorders: A Guide for Clinicians and Their Clients,
First Edition. Greta Noordenbos.
© 2013 John Wiley & Sons, Ltd. Published 2013 by John Wiley & Sons, Ltd.

Although the first steps on the path to recovery were very difficult, they finally succeeded to eat in a healthy way and to enjoy food. They developed a positive attitude towards their body, had better self-esteem, and were able to express their emotions and have a worthwhile social life. They were very proud of having overcome their eating disorder. This is very clear from what Caroline says:

> Each new day I am so glad to be alive and I really enjoy my life. It is a great pleasure to go to work, and to feel the wind in my hair when I walk or bike. I have much more energy and enjoy each ray of sunshine on my skin. I now see food as a rich source of energy and I really like it, instead of being scared of it. I am also grateful to my lovely friends and parents. The way to recovery was not easy and sometimes I almost lost the courage to continue, but the reward is very high. I really hope that all people who struggle with an eating disorder are able to recover, because they have so much to gain.

The experiences of recovered patients offer much hope, as they show that full recovery is possible. Their stories make clear that the process of recovery is not easy, but the result is worthwhile. This should inspire people who continue to struggle with eating disorders and therapists who try to help them recover.

When have Eating Disorder Patients Recovered?

In the literature on recovery from eating disorders, it is difficult to find a clear definition of recovery (Noordenbos, 2011). For a long time, the criteria for recovery from an eating disorder were restricted to the reduction of symptoms, such as disturbed eating habits and weight. However, even when these symptoms have alleviated, the underlying factors remain. As long as these factors are not addressed, the risk of relapse is quite high. Strober, Freeman, and Morrell (1997) evaluate the reduction of symptoms as *partial recovery*. For *full recovery* from an eating disorder, not only should the symptoms be reduced, but the underlying factors which have contributed to the development of the eating disorder should also be alleviated. Full recovery implies eating the right amount of food and maintaining a healthy weight, having a positive body attitude, increased self-esteem, and better emotional and social coping strategies (Björk & Ahlström, 2008; Deter, 1992; Noordenbos, 2011; Noordenbos & Seubring, 2006; Pettersen & Rosenvinge, 2002). Moreover, *co-morbidity* also needs to be reduced, such as alcohol abuse, depression, fear disorders, personality disorders, and so on (Steinhausen, 2002).

Research shows that most patients can recover quite well from their eating disorder, and full recovery is possible for many patients. In general, 50% of the patients with anorexia and bulimia nervosa recover, 30%

improve and 20% stay ill (Steinhausen, 1999, 2002). The percentage of patients who recover from bulimia is somewhat higher and those who recover from binge eating disorder is even more so. Recently, the percentage of patients who have recovered has increased because of earlier diagnosis and better treatment. In case of adolescents, eating disorder recovery percentages are as high as 85% (Nilsson & Hagglöf, 2006).

Can All Patients Recover from their Eating Disorder?

Unfortunately, not all patients can recover from their eating disorder. Factors that severely hamper their recovery are a late diagnosis, patient's and doctor's delay, late and inadequate treatment which focuses only on partial recovery such as food and weight increase, combined with a lack of attention to the reduction of the underlying factors, lack of aftercare and no strategies to prevent relapses. The longer patients have had an eating disorder, the more difficult it is to change their eating habits and to reduce the physical, psychological and social consequences. When treatment is not adequate and effective, patients lose their hope of improvement and recovery (Noordenbos, Oldenhave, Muschter, & Terpstra, 2002). However, this book shows that even after many years of having had an eating disorder, patients were able to improve the quality of their lives and some were able to recover.

Recovered Patients as Guides and Role Models

In this book, many former patients talk about the process of recovering from their eating disorder. Although most of the patients quoted are female, there are also some male patients who tell us about their recovery process. To preserve patients' privacy, their names have been changed.

All recovered patients sooner or later found a way out of the prison of their disorder. They talk about the stages they have gone through and all the adjustments they had to make in order to recover. They also tell us about the problems, traps and pitfalls they had to overcome and how they survived. Their stories are the best evidence that it is possible to recover from an eating disorder. Recovered patients, whether female or male, are therefore role models for all those who continue to struggle with their eating disorder.

Content of the Book

This book begins by describing the most important stages in the development of eating disorders, from problems and risk factors in the period before the actual start of the eating disorder (Chapter 1) to the first stage of dieting and slimming, which is often experienced as very positive (Chapter 2). However, patients are soon confronted with all kinds of negative psychological, physical and social consequences, which are described in Chapter 3. When the negative consequences become very severe and dominate patients' lives, they reach a turning point after which they feel motivated to recover, as described in Chapter 4.

The process of changing eating habits and overcoming the fear of a healthy diet is described in Chapter 5, and the development of a more positive body attitude is dealt with in Chapter 6. In Chapter 7, the process of recovering from all negative physical consequences is described, while Chapter 8 deals with the development of self-esteem and a more positive self-evaluation. Chapter 9 focuses on how patients learn to express their emotions and feelings. Chapter 10 deals with how patients developed better social relations. In Chapter 11, the most relevant questions about recovery are answered. In the final chapter, Chapter 12, a checklist for all relevant aspects of recovery is presented.

A Book for Both Clinicians and Clients

This book is important for all therapists and professionals who work with eating disorder patients. It offers them a clear insight into the changes which are necessary in order to recover from an eating disorder, such as normalizing eating habits and weight, increasing self-esteem and body attitude, and learning to express emotions and develop better social relations.

This book will be very useful for all those who struggle with an eating disorder, whether they be female or male, have just been afflicted by their eating disorder, or have already had an eating disorder for many years. They can be motivated to change when they read the stories of former patients who succeeded in recovering from their eating disorder. Recovered patients are the best guides to show the way out of the prison of the disorder. Eating disorder patients will find many assignments and questionnaires in this book which can help them overcome their eating disorder.

This book will also be very informative for parents and friends, who may learn from it not only why this disorder is so difficult to overcome, but also that full recovery is possible.

How Therapists and other Professionals may Use this Book

Therapists and other professionals who work with eating disorder patients can use this book as a guide to help their patients in the recovery process. You can follow this book together with your clients. You can ask them to take up the tests and assignments in this book and discuss the results. This book will help your clients to talk about their problems in the period before their eating disorder and about their reasons to start dieting. You can have an insight into all the consequences of their eating disorder. They may even be motivated to change when they fill in the questionnaires about motivation to recover. In the following chapters, there are all kinds of assignments for the client in order to normalize their eating habits, to develop a positive body attitude, to recover from the physical consequences of the eating disorder, to develop more self-esteem and a positive identity, to learn to express emotions and to improve social relationships.

In order to take up the tests and assignments in this book, it is important that your clients use a *diary* or a *notebook*. Although the information in a diary is often meant to remain secret, you should make it clear to your patients that you will discuss the tests and assignments with them in order to support them in their recovery process.

This book is not a protocol and can be used in a flexible way, depending on the stage of recovery your client is in. Moreover, this book can be combined with all kinds of treatments such as self-help groups, group therapy, cognitive behavioural therapy, interpersonal therapy, acceptance and commitment therapy or compassion-focused therapy.

For full recovery, it is essential that all relevant goals in this book are realized: normalizing eating habits, developing a positive body attitude, recovering from the physical consequences, developing more self-esteem and a positive identity, learning to express emotions and improving social relationships. Chapter 12 contains a checklist for recovery which can help you find out which criteria have already been realized and which criteria need more attention.

How Eating Disorder Patients may Use this Book

If you have an eating disorder, it is often very difficult to admit that you have severe problems, and even more difficult to accept that you need help. In this book, you can read about many patients who have recovered: they had the same problems but were able to overcome them. They are the best guides out of the prison of the eating disorder and important role models for recovery. You can read this book alone, but it might be helpful to ask a therapist or clinician to support you on your way to recovery.

It is useful to *buy a diary* or *notebook* in which you can write down your experiences, feelings and thoughts about having an eating disorder and discuss them with your therapist. In this book, you will find several assignments which you can answer in your diary or notebook. The results can be discussed with your therapist. With the support of your therapist, this book will help you recover step by step from your eating disorder.

How Parents, Partners and Friends may Use this Book

This book provides a great deal of information about and insight into the behaviour, thoughts and feelings of your child, partner or friend who has developed an eating disorder. It makes it clear that an eating disorder is a severe problem from which it is not easy to recover. It is therefore very important to motivate patients to find professional treatment.

At the same time, the book offers hope and sends a positive message, because many former patients show that it is possible to recover from an eating disorder. They reveal the importance of changing their eating habits, recovering from the negative physical consequences, developing more self-esteem and a positive body attitude, learning to express their emotions and improving their social relations. Your support as a parent, partner or friend is very important for their recovery process.

1

Problems in the Period before the Eating Disorder

Introduction

To understand why recovery from an eating disorder is so difficult and takes so much time, it is important to understand how and why the eating disorder developed in the first place.

Eating disorders never come *out of the blue*; they are preceded by many problems and risk factors (Fairburn et al., 1997; Jacobi, de Zwaan, Hayward, Kraemer, & Agras, 2004; Stice, 2002; Striegel-Moore & Bulik, 2007). The risk factors can be divided into genetic and biological, psychological and socio-cultural factors. These factors make patients vulnerable to starting a diet and developing a disturbed eating pattern which can result in an eating disorder.

Many eating disorder patients have family members who have or have had an affective disorder such as depression, alcohol problems, drug addiction or an eating disorder (Keel, 2005). Although these genetic factors never predict the development of an eating disorder, they make the person more vulnerable than people without these risk factors.

The psychological risk factors mentioned most often by eating disorder patients are low self-esteem and negative self- and body-evaluation (Cervera et al., 2003; Noordenbos, 2007). Perfectionism and fear of failing in the eyes of others are also important risk factors for developing an eating disorder (Jacobi et al., 2004). Eating disorder patients set high standards for themselves and feel that they have failed when they do not achieve their goals. A major risk factor is having a negative body attitude and the fear of becoming overweight or fat. Negative comments about their body or being teased about their weight and appearance are important factors in the development of a

Recovery from Eating Disorders: A Guide for Clinicians and Their Clients,
First Edition. Greta Noordenbos.
© 2013 John Wiley & Sons, Ltd. Published 2013 by John Wiley & Sons, Ltd.

negative body attitude. Sociocultural factors, such as the slimming ideal and dieting behaviour of mothers, sisters and friends or strict weight standards in ballet schools and in sports such as skating and athletics in which weight plays an important role (Levine & Smolak, 1998; Pinhas, Toner, Garfinkel, & Stuckless, 1999), can also contribute to these negative feelings.

Risk factors, however, are never predictors for eating disorders, but only increase vulnerability. Moreover, no single risk factor is in itself enough to develop an eating disorder; the more the risk factors, the greater the possibility of starting to diet in a culture where being slim is the ideal for the female body. What were the most important risk factors which preceded former patients' eating disorder?

Lack of Self-Esteem and Negative Self-Evaluation

The psychological problems mentioned most often by eating disorder patients are lack of self-esteem and negative self-evaluation (Noordenbos, 2007). Because of their low self-esteem, they feel insecure about themselves and need support from others. In order to receive approval and support, they do their best to comply with the expectations of others. However, they are very insecure about their own opinions and find it difficult to express their own thoughts and feelings, as they want to avoid any criticism. They do their best not to be criticized by others, because they experience censure as rejection. This is clearly described in the following quote:

> ANGELIQUE: 'I was strongly dependent on the approval of others and tried to avoid any criticism or negative comments, because I was very afraid of not being accepted. When I got critical remarks from others I had the feeling that I was being completely rejected. In order to prevent other persons from having a negative opinion about me or criticizing me I always did my best to comply with their expectations.'

Compliant and Pleasing Behaviour

In the period before the development of an eating disorder, many patients are kind and obedient children who do their best at school and at home. However, at the root of this compliant behaviour is the fear of not being able to cope with the expectations of their parents and teachers. According to Bruch (1978), they do not feel that they may be who they are, and hence they try to comply with the image they think others have of them. When they try to comply, they receive approval and affirmation and feel accepted.

Pleasing behaviour is very often found in anorectic patients. The famous author Jane Fonda therefore labels anorexia nervosa as 'the disease to please.'

Patients spend most of their time trying to discover what other persons expect from them because of their low self-esteem and need for support and acceptance. However, this prevents them from exploring their own feelings and opinions and expressing these to others. The following quotation from one of Bruch's patients clearly shows how much she conformed to others:

> I was sitting with these three people but I felt a terrible fragmentation of myself. There wasn't a person inside at all. I tried with whoever I was with to reflect the image they had of me, to do what they expected me to do. There were three different people, I had to be a different person to each, and I had to balance that. It was the same when I was a child and had friends. It was always in response to what they wanted (Bruch, 1978, p. 49).

In the period before the eating disorder, patients often struggle with the following questions: What do other people think of me? Do they like me? How do I have to behave in order to be accepted? How can I prevent people from criticizing or rejecting me? In order to be accepted, they always try to adjust to the expectations of others, hiding their own feelings and opinions (Miller, 1981).

Hiding Real Thoughts and Opinions from others

Children who suffer from lack of self-esteem, insecurity and fear of failure often try to adapt to the expectations of their parents and teachers in order to be accepted. They are afraid to express their real feelings and opinions and hide them from others when they feel these views might be different from what others feel or think. They adjust to others as much as possible and feel valued for their pleasing behaviour. Much before the development of their eating disorder, they learn that their outward behaviour and appearance is important to gain approval from others, and they hide their inner insecurity and negative feelings as much as possible.

ANN: 'When I was a teenager I always tried to hide my real inner feelings from others. By adjusting to the expectations of my parents and teachers I hoped to be accepted and valued. I always did my best at school and tried to be the perfect daughter. Unfortunately I did not realize that my pleasing behaviour did not bring me what I really longed for: attention and acceptance of my real self.'

Sensitivity to the Needs of others

Many patients told me that in the period before the development of their eating disorder, they were very sensitive to the needs and feelings of others. They were able to register subtle signals from their parents, especially signals of sorrow, disappointment, anger, depression, fear or stress.

This is clearly described by Hilde Bruch (1978): 'They try to fulfil the needs of others as best they can and do their best to give no problems. This psychological worrying about their parents and especially their mothers makes that they feel obliged to help their mothers as much as possible and to be the sunshine in their home.'

However, being so sensitive to the expectations and needs of others often has a price: patients learn to neglect their own needs and feelings. They become experts in caring about others, but do not learn to express their own needs, hiding their problems from their parents. When one of their parents is unable to fulfil the emotional needs of the other parent, they try to compensate; but behind this adjusting and pleasing behaviour is a deep lack of self-esteem.

> LINDA: 'I remember clearly that during my puberty I worried much about my mother, who was very ill and finally died of cancer. I felt so much sorrow for her ongoing decline and her disappointment when the treatment was not successful. I also saw how my father suffered because of my mother's cancer. I tried to fulfil their needs as much as possible and suppressed my own troubles and need for attention. I could not blame them for not spending enough attention on me. But I became more and more depressed and felt very lonely and empty with all my sad feelings, knowing that my mother would die of her cancer. For that reason I never dared to ask attention for my own emotions and show my feelings of disappointment, sorrow, or anger. I felt very alone, but I could not blame my parents because they had so many serious problems and were completely absorbed by their own feelings of sorrow.'

Patients with bulimia nervosa often say that they felt emotionally empty, because their parents never asked how they felt. In order to comfort them-selves and to suppress their negative and sad feelings, they developed binges.

> MARY: 'As soon as I got feelings of distress I started to eat in order to avoid and suppress them. But even after a huge binge my feeling of hunger never went away and I never felt really satisfied. It felt as if there was a huge hole around my hearth and stomach. I was really longing for emotional comfort, and the only way I could comfort myself was by eating plenty of food.'

Perfectionism and Fear of Failure

In the period before the eating disorder, anorectic patients are often extreme perfectionists. They set very high standards for themselves and are never satisfied with their performances. They feel they are not good enough and always think they need to be better. At school, they try to please their parents and teachers by doing their best and aiming for the highest grades.

SUZAN: 'at home I always wanted to be the most loved child, and in school I wanted to be the best student. I really needed to hear from my parents that I did my best and to be valued for that, because I felt so insecure about myself. I was often afraid that I did something wrong and my parents would no longer love me. When I received a high grade in school I felt reassured for a short time, but always was afraid I would fail the next time, and my parents would be disappointed with my performances.'

Even when they always have high grades, patients often feel that this is not good enough.

NATASCHA: 'When I made even the smallest mistake, there was always a critical voice in my head that said: "you did not do your best, everybody can see that you made mistakes and that you failed".'

Inner Criticism and Negative Self-Evaluation

Eating disorder patients are often very critical about themselves. This self-criticism already starts in the period before they start to diet, but increases when they have developed an eating disorder. This inner criticism is described by several therapists, such as Bruch (1978), as an 'inner dictator'; Claude-Pierre (1997) refers to this as an 'inner negativist' and Kortink (2008) labels it as an 'inner saboteur.'

It is especially children who are very insecure about themselves who run the risk of developing this inner criticism and negative self-evaluation. They have a very strict superego and high standards and blame themselves for every mistake.

Some patients had parents who were very critical of them and expected high grades and excellent performances from their children. When they internalized this attitude of their parents, they learnt to look at themselves in a very critical way. They began to have unreasonable expectations from themselves and were never satisfied with their performances.

CAROL: 'For my examinations I always did my best, because I knew that my grades were very important for my father. He pushed me to have an 8 or 9. I still can remember those times that I had a 7.5 for a very difficult examination. When I went home I felt very bad about myself: I already saw the disappointed face of my father and heard his voice: "Why a 7.5? Didn't you study hard enough? You might have worked harder! You can get an 8 or even a 9". After this kind of rebuke he would open his newspaper, leaving me alone with all my negative feelings. Even years later, when I lived on campus, I still heard my father's voice criticizing me for not having done my best.'

Most eating disorder patients experience their inner critical thoughts as a result of their own high standards. In the severe stage of their eating disorder, however, they sometimes hear an inner negative *voice* in their head which has got out of their control (Bruch, 1978; Noordenbos, Boesenach, Moerman, & Trommelen, 2012; Tierney & Fox, 2010).

BEA: 'In the period when I had severe anorexia nervosa I continually heard that critical voice in my head, always censuring me. It was as if I had the voice of an inner dictator in my head and after each small bit of food I heard the voice saying: "that was too much, you were not allowed to eat that, now you have to be punished, and you cannot have dinner, because you already ate too much today". It was terrible to hear that voice all day long and it was utterly impossible to resist it. This inner critical voice made me very unhappy and depressed.'

How can we explain eating disorder patients hearing a negative critical voice? A possible explanation might be that they start by developing very strict eating habits, which act as their inner conscience or superego. The more extreme their diet and the more undernourished their body, the more dominant their inner critical thoughts. Finally these inner critical thoughts are heard as an autonomous voice in their heads, which grows louder and louder (Heffner & Eifert, 2004). Some patients experience their inner voice as a very demanding superego, which completely dominates their wishes and needs.

ANN: 'I was completely dependent on the mercy of my inner negative voice, which undermined all my self-esteem. Nothing was good enough. Everything I did was wrong and could have been done better.'

Impaired Identity Development

Developing their own identity is a long process in the development of young people. Psychologists describe several stages in this process (Erikson, 1968). Around the age of 3 most children go through a stage of obstinacy, in which they learn to say 'no' to their parents. During puberty, they start to rebel against their parents, and during adolescence they try to separate themselves from their parents and become independent individuals with their own identity, values, thoughts and opinions.

Stages in the ego and identity development

---

3 years: obstinacy – learning to say 'no'
12 years: puberty – rebelling against parents
18 years: adolescence – developing independence and own identity

---

Not all children, however, go through these stages. They can stagnate somewhere along the way. The more insecure they are, the more sensitive they will be to the expectations of others, and the more difficult it is for them to develop their own identity. They often try to please their parents and to adapt to their expectations, thus curbing their rebellious nature and impeding the development of their own identity.

> GRACE: 'In the period before my eating disorder I was very afraid of having conflicts with my parents and I tried to avoid them as much as possible. If I had an opinion that differed from theirs I was afraid that my parents might criticize me and not accept my opinion.'

In order to be able to express one's own opinions, it is important to have enough self-esteem. Eating disorder patients, however, have low self-esteem. They prefer to avoid conflicts and hide their opinions and feelings from others, because they are afraid of being criticized and rejected.

When parents are insecure and have low self-esteem, they are not able to stimulate their children to develop self-esteem and to become assertive. Lack of self-esteem can become a trans-generational problem, passed from one generation to the next.

> RUTH: 'My mother was very insecure and had little self-esteem, especially in the period when she divorced my father. I always felt the need to support my mother, but this made it very difficult for me to express my own feelings and opinions and to develop my own identity and so become more independent of my mother.'

Negative Body Attitude

Negative self-evaluation in the period before the eating disorder is often strongly related to a negative body evaluation. The more negative patients think about themselves, the more negative they think about their body.

Many girls, especially during puberty, when they develop more fat tissue around their hips, grow breasts and start to menstruate, become insecure about and critical of their body. For many girls, menstruation is not a pleasant experience, because it is often combined with stomach ache, a blown-up feeling and a tension in the breasts. When girls have low self-esteem, every comment about their physique is felt as negative. This can easily trigger the wish to change their body in order to reduce their negative body image.

It is not only the development of the body during puberty that makes girls insecure about their body, but also the pictures of *ideal* models who are very thin. These photographs are often the result of a combined effort from many *beaufyers* such as cosmeticians, hairdressers, stylists for clothes and shoes, and finally substantial adaptations on the computer. Girls who are insecure about themselves can become sensitive to pictures of slim models and tend to compare their own body with the ideal. If they have friends, sisters or parents who diet, the pressure to slim down can become very high. A special risk group are ballet dancers or athletes who need to stay below a certain weight in order to be successful (Piran, 1999).

In a culture in which being slim is seen as the ideal, being overweight is viewed in a very negative light. One critical comment can sometimes be enough to trigger dieting.

> MONIQUE: 'When we were at the swimming pool one of my schoolmates said to me in front of many others: "look, you have a real paunch!" At that moment I wished I could disappear. This was the trigger for me to start a diet.'

Many eating disorder patients told me that they were teased about their weight or figure.

> DAPHNE: 'I was always a bit overweight but when I went to secondary school I got many negative comments about my weight. They called me Fatty, Fatso, Billy Bunter, etcetera. I felt very bad and decided to get rid of that fat as soon as possible.'

Not all patients had the same problems in the period before they developed an eating disorder.

The following questionnaire may help to get an insight into the factors and problems which preceded your eating disorder.

Questionnaire about problems in the period before the eating disorder

What problems did you have in the period before you started to diet and developed an eating disorder? Answer the questions with yes or no.

Questions about problems and risk factors

1. Do you have family members who have (had) an eating disorder?
2. Do you have family members who have been depressed?
3. Do you have family members who have been addicted to alcohol or drugs?
4. Do you have low self-esteem?
5. Are you very alert to the needs of others?
6. Do you hide your emotions and feelings?
7. Do you set high standards for yourself?
8. Are you afraid of failing or of not being able to fulfil other people's expectations of you?
9. Are you afraid of not being accepted or of being rejected by others?
10. Are you afraid of being criticized?
11. Do you have a negative body attitude?
12. Are you afraid of becoming overweight or obese?
13. Do you receive negative comments about your weight?
14. Have you been teased about your weight, figure or appearance?
15. Do you have family members or friends who have been dieting?
16. Has somebody advised you to lose weight or to follow a diet?
17. Did you have other problems in the period before you started dieting?

Other problems were
....
....

After filling out this form, you can discuss your answers with your therapist in order to get better insight into the problems you had in the period before your eating disorder.

Summary

In the period before the development of an eating disorder, many risk factors can increase patients' vulnerability, such as genetic factors, lack of self-esteem, being overly sensitive to the needs of others, being unable to express emotions, perfectionism, fear of failure, negative body evaluation or being teased about their weight. Because of insecurity and a lack of self-esteem, much approval and support from others is needed. Patients therefore try to please others and to adjust to the expectations others have of them. The opinion of other people is very important for their self-image and self-esteem. At school, they do their best and are perfectionists. They set very high standards for themselves and feel that they have failed when they are not able to fulfil their expectations.

Because of their fear of criticism, they find it difficult to express their thoughts and opinions and hide them from others.

Negative self-evaluation is often related to a negative body evaluation, especially during puberty when body weight increases. When patients are confronted with the slim body ideal and feel under pressure to lose weight, they become motivated to start a diet. Girls and boys who are teased about their figure or weight and who develop a very negative view of their body are especially at risk of starting a diet. Dieting is often the first stage in the development of an eating disorder. However, not all people who start dieting develop an eating disorder. What makes patients continue their diet in such an extreme way that they develop an eating disorder? That process will be described in Chapter 2.

2

First Stage: Extreme Dieting

Introduction

Although eating disorder patients mostly start to diet in order to lose weight, not all people who diet develop an eating disorder. There are significant differences between persons who diet in a healthy way and those who diet at an extreme level, which is a high risk factor for developing an eating disorder. Those who diet at an extreme level have significantly more problems in the period before they start to diet and have unrealistically high expectations about losing weight. They see their slimming behaviour as a *solution* for their psychological problems. Dieting and weight loss give them self-esteem, control and positive feelings about themselves. This positive evaluation motivates them to continue their slimming behaviour even after considerable weight loss. In this chapter, former eating disorder patients recount how they started to diet at an extreme level and how they viewed their slimming behaviour in the first stage of their eating disorder.

How does an Eating Disorder Start?

It is difficult to say exactly when and how eating disorders start, but most patients mention the decision to diet in order to lose weight as the starting point of their disorder. Dieting can be triggered by many factors, such as weight increase, critical remarks about one's figure or being teased about one's weight. Other triggers for dieting are negative experiences such as

Recovery from Eating Disorders: A Guide for Clinicians and Their Clients,
First Edition. Greta Noordenbos.
© 2013 John Wiley & Sons, Ltd. Published 2013 by John Wiley & Sons, Ltd.

not being accepted by peers, feelings of loss or traumatic experiences such as the severe illness or death of a parent or physical and sexual abuse. Nearly all eating disorder patients say that before this trigger, they already had a negative self-evaluation and body attitude. When they got negative comments about their body or had negative life experiences, their self-evaluation and view of their body became even more negative. In order to improve their negative body image and self-assessment, they decided to diet.

Developing an eating disorder is not comparable to getting influenza. In the case of influenza, one can feel healthy the day before and yet wake up with a headache, sore throat and fever the next morning. An eating disorder, however, does not develop within a few days. It never comes out of the blue, but is preceded by a long period of problems before the decision to start a diet (Bruch, 1978; Jacobi, de Zwaan, Hayward, Kraemer, & Agras, 2004; Stice, 2002). The triggers for dieting can be quite diverse, such as increased weight so that clothes do not fit any more, negative comments about one's weight, being teased about one's figure or negative sexual experiences.

Suzy was always very insecure and afraid to fail. She often felt that she was not good enough. She started to diet after she had been jumping on a trampoline together with a classmate and received nasty comments about her weight.

SUZY: 'Others observed that the trampoline was lower when I jumped than when my classmate jumped. When they asked about our weights it turned out I weighed one kilo or two pounds more than my classmate. I really felt bad about that. I concluded that my weight was too high and I decided to start a diet in order to lose at least one kilo. I did not realize that I weighed more because I was taller than my classmate. But the comment about my weight was the trigger for me to start to diet in a rigorous way.'

Many girls and boys are teased about their weight before they decide to diet. In her diary about her anorexia nervosa period, Natasha van Weezel (2006) describes how some of her classmates called her 'Fatty'. Her decision was clear: 'I am going to lose weight as soon as possible.'

Sometimes weight loss precedes the decision to diet, for example in case of severe stress or a disease. When patients view the weight loss as positive, they become motivated to continue dieting in a more extreme way. Although the diet often starts with a conscious decision to lose weight, it is never their intention to develop anorexia or bulimia nervosa. Developing an eating disorder is a gradual process in which thinking about weight and food slowly takes possession of the patient's mind.

Table 2.1   Differences in dieting behaviour between healthy and extreme dieters.

Reasons given by women who diet in a healthy way	Additional reasons given by women who diet in an extreme way
1. My clothes did not fit any more	8. I want to develop more self-esteem
2. I want to lose a few kilos or pounds	9. I want to develop more self-respect
3. I want to go down two clothes sizes	10. I want to feel more accepted
4. I want to feel more fit	11. I do not want to be teased any longer
5. I do not want to feel fat	12. I want to overcome my shyness
6. I want to eat healthier food	13. I want more control over my body
7. I want to become more attractive	14. I want to become happier

Differences Between Healthy and Extreme Dieters

Although the first period of dieting of eating disorder patients does not differ from the dieting behaviour of healthy dieters, there are significant differences in their expectations regarding losing weight. These differences are presented in Table 2.1. The left-hand column lists the reasons for dieting mentioned by women who just want to lose some weight and stop when they reach their target weight. These reasons were also given by eating disorder patients, but they mentioned psychological and social reasons to diet more often. These additional reasons are given in the right-hand column (Noordenbos, 2007).

For eating disorder patients, the psychological and social reasons for dieting as mentioned in the second column were very important. They hoped that losing weight might change their negative feelings about themselves and their body. The first weight loss was experienced as very positive and their self-esteem increased substantially.

Questions about your reasons for going on a diet

What were the most important reasons to start dieting? You can answer:

1 = not at all, 2 = very little, 3 = somewhat, 4 = much, or 5 = very strong

1.	My clothes did not fit any longer	1	2	3	4	5
2.	I will lose a few kilos or pounds	1	2	3	4	5
3.	I will go down two clothes sizes	1	2	3	4	5
4.	I will feel more fit	1	2	3	4	5
5.	I will not feel fat	1	2	3	4	5
6.	I will eat healthier food	1	2	3	4	5
7.	I will become more attractive	1	2	3	4	5
8.	I will develop more self-esteem	1	2	3	4	5
9.	I will feel more accepted	1	2	3	4	5

10.	I will no longer be teased	1	2	3	4	5
11.	I will become less shy	1	2	3	4	5
12.	I will develop more self-respect	1	2	3	4	5
13.	I will be happier	1	2	3	4	5
14.	I will have more control over my body	1	2	3	4	5

Other reasons:

15.	....	1	2	3	4	5
16.	....	1	2	3	4	5
17.	....	1	2	3	4	5
18.	....	1	2	3	4	5
19.	....	1	2	3	4	5
20.	....	1	2	3	4	5

After you have filled in this questionnaire, you can discuss your answers with your therapist.

The topics you have answered with 3, 4 or 5 would require special attention in your treatment.

From Healthy to Extreme Dieting

Although eating disorder patients often started dieting in a healthy way, they sooner or later went on to extreme dieting (Noordenbos, 2007). The differences between healthy and extreme dieting are listed in Table 2.2.

Table 2.2   Differences between healthy and extreme dieting.

Healthy dieting	Extreme dieting
1. Fewer sweets and snacks	1. No sweets and snacks
2. Less fat and sugar	2. No fat and sugar
3. Smaller portions of food	3. Very small portions
4. More vegetables and less potatoes or pasta	4. Very few or no potatoes, pasta or meat
5. More fruit and fewer snacks	5. Only fruit and vegetables
6. Three meals, three light snacks	6. Skipping meals and snacks
7. Moderate exercising	7. Intense exercising
8. Target weight is healthy for age and height	8. Target weight is very low for age and height
9. Not obsessed by food and weight	9. Obsessed by food and weight loss
10. Dieting stops after target weight has been reached	10. Dieting continues even after considerable weight loss

Although most eating disorder patients start off with a healthy diet, they sooner or later start to diet in a very extreme way, which is a high risk factor for developing an eating disorder (Stice, 2002).

Questions about your dieting patterns

What is your dieting pattern? Please circle all answers which describe your eating habits:

1. I eat fewer sweets and snacks
2. I eat less fat and sugar
3. I eat smaller portions of food
4. I eat more vegetables and less potatoes, pasta and meat
5. I eat more fruit and fewer snacks
6. I eat three meals and three light snacks
7. I exercise more often
8. I have a target weight which is healthy for my age and height
9. I am not obsessed by food and weight
10. I want to stop dieting after realizing my target weight
11. I no longer eat any sweets and snacks
12. I eat no fat and sugar
13. I eat very small portions
14. I eat very few potatoes, little pasta and meat
15. I eat no potatoes, pasta and meat
16. I eat only vegetables and fruit
17. I skip meals and snacks
18. I exercise very often
19. I eat less to have a low weight
20. I often think about food and weight
21. I continue my diet even after considerable weight loss
22. My meals are very irregular
23. I do not have breakfast
24. I do not have lunch
25. I have no snacks between my meals
26. I have binges
27. I vomit after food intake
28. I use laxatives
29. I use diuretics
30. I use slimming pills
31. Do you have any other strategies to lose weight?

....

....

....

Your answers give more insight into your slimming behaviour and are important for your treatment.

Why Continue Dieting?

One of the most striking characteristics of anorexia nervosa is the continuation of extreme dieting even after considerable weight loss. This is very difficult to understand for parents, friends and therapists. When we ask anorexia patients why they continue to diet, they say that slimming behaviour gives them positive feelings of self-esteem and control over their lives.

> HELENA: 'Being successful in dieting and weight loss gave me much self-esteem and strong feelings of control. I had the feeling that I had given a special performance. While people around me got worried about my slimming behaviour and saw all kinds of problems, I felt that I had found a very good solution for all the negative feelings I had before I started to diet, such as a severe lack of self-esteem, fear of failure and a negative body view. When I started to diet I felt I had found a strategy to manage these problems. Extreme dieting gave me self-esteem and control. Before dieting I felt no control over my life, and now I managed to control my food intake and weight. For the first time in my life I felt very strong and proud of myself.'

Extreme dieting substantially increases patients' self-esteem:

> SHEILA: 'When I succeeded in losing weight, I literally started to feel weighty' (MacLeod, 1981).
>
> ANN: 'Dieting and slimming is what I can do much better than others. That makes me feel very strong, much stronger than all those people who are not able to continue their diet.'

Some anorexia patients feel very proud of themselves:

> DEBBY: 'When I was still able to refuse food even when I was hungry I felt superior compared to all those persons who could not continue their diet. The more weight I lost the more I felt I was on the right way. I wanted to be famous because I was so special and I wanted people to have respect for what I did.'
>
> SARAH: 'By extreme dieting I could show other people that I was very strong, and that I was able to continue my slimming behaviour.'

Some anorexia patients said that they often felt hungry, but they saw this as something positive rather than negative. They felt good when their stomach was empty.

CAROLINE: 'That I was able to endure my feelings of hunger and to lose weight motivated me to continue my slimming behaviour. This positive self-evaluation was very important for me and I did not want to lose that feeling. For that reason I was afraid to gain weight, because then I might fail so that my positive self-evaluation might collapse. For that reason gaining weight had to be prevented at any price, because my thin body was my pride and identity. Not gaining weight became the most important goal in my life.'

Hilde Bruch (1978) has described very clearly how anorectic patients feel and think. They feel great, and would feel very guilty, or even get the idea they were repellent, if they gained as much as an ounce. Because of their starvation, they can no longer view themselves realistically. Their emaciation is their top performance, and they are very proud about that.

This positive self-evaluation is very important for them and stimulates them to neglect their feelings of hunger. They absolutely cling to their feeling of control about food and weight, as described in the diary of Natascha van Weezel (2006).

NATASCHA: 'To lose weight was the only thing I excelled at, the only thing I really could manage. My only gift should not be spoiled. It gave me a very good feeling that I was able to continue my extreme diet, a kick of adrenaline. I started to realize that I was very good at slimming and finally found something to show my will power.'

GABY: 'For the first time in my life I was able to say "no" and to stop complying with the expectations of others. I felt I was developing a strong feeling of "self" and control, which gave me great self-esteem.'

LISA: 'When I started dieting I had for the first time in my life the feeling that I could control something. Positive reactions from other people stimulated me to continue my diet in an extreme way. This was what I was very good at. Extreme dieting gave me a feeling of "self" and "identity". I felt I had become an independent person who no longer obeyed my parents. That felt great.'

Eating Disorder or Identity Disorder?

Many eating disorder patients report that the first stage of dieting gave them very positive feelings and a strong sense of self and identity. This positive view of extreme dieting makes it very difficult for them to stop their regime, because they are afraid of losing control over their food and weight again, and to lose their positive self-image and feelings of identity.

FARIDAH: 'I remember quite well that I was scared to eat and to gain weight, because all my feelings of identity would completely disappear and nothing would be left of myself.'

The term *eating disorder* suggests that eating habit is the core problem, but patients' eating habits are strongly related to their self-evaluation. In the DSM-IV (APA, 2000), too, the connection between food regulation and self-evaluation is mentioned as one of the core criteria for anorexia and bulimia nervosa. Criterion C for anorexia nervosa and criterion D for bulimia nervosa in the DSM-IV both state that self-evaluation is unduly influenced by body shape and weight. An interesting question is whether an eating disorder can be seen as an identity disorder.

According to Bruch (1978), anorexia nervosa is a consequence of an impaired development of identity and individualization. Before the development of anorexia nervosa, there is a strong tendency to conform to the expectations of others and to hide one's own feelings, needs and emotions. Because of their impaired self-esteem and lack of identity, they feel very dependent on others. When they reach puberty and adolescence, they feel the need for more autonomy and to become independent from their parents. However, they discover that their identity is impaired. When they start to diet, they feel they are developing their own identity and are proud to have control over their food and weight. This gives them very positive feelings about themselves.

Control over Food and Body

Some eating disorder patients experience the development of female sexual characteristics such as breasts and menstruation as very negative. The sexual development of their body makes them feel out of control. By dieting and reducing weight, they are able to stop their body from developing. In particular, girls who have had negative sexual experiences or have been sexually abused use extreme slimming as a way to desexualize their body.

As a consequence of extreme dieting and weight loss, all kinds of negative emotions disappear. Some eating disorder patients feel completely dissociated from their body and their physical needs. According to Bruch (1978), some anorectic patients experience their body and mind as two separate entities, with the mind having the task of controlling the despised body.

Some anorectic patients impose extreme ascetic rules upon themselves, which enables them to neglect all needs and feelings of their body such as hunger, cold and pain. Being able to control their body gives them a feeling of power over their physical needs.

In spite of the weakness associated with such a severe weight loss, they will drive themselves to unbelievable feats to demonstrate that they live by the idea of "mind over body" (Bruch, 1978, p. 5).

Controlling their body becomes an ultimate performance. They behave like a tyrant who has absolute power over their body. In their way of thinking they are not allowed to be indulgent towards the needs of their body. Even when the feeling of hunger is very severe, they see their ability to delay even the smallest bite as a victory of their mind over their body. This makes them feel proud. But when they fail they develop severe feelings of guilt and self-reproach. They experience their failure as a sin in which they indulged the vulgar needs of their despised body, and condemn themselves to even less food and more hunger (Bruch, 1978, p. 62).

According to Bruch (1978), hunger is not the only physical demand that is denied, because not giving in to fatigue rates equally high.

Swimming one more lap, running one more mile, doing ever more excruciating calisthenics, everything becomes a symbol of victory over the body. Not wearing a coat in the midst of winter or swimming in cold water that makes the skin turn blue is valued for the same reason, though one of the distressing by-effects of starvation is unusual sensitivity to cold. The body and its demands have to be subjugated every day, hour, and minute (Bruch, 1978, pp. 62/63).

Extreme dieting results in patients becoming more and more obsessed by food and weight. Their thoughts become bizarre, and they develop absurd ideas about food. They can think of nothing else and become completely occupied with thoughts about food and weight. Their eating habits become a trap from which it is difficult to escape.

Denial of Problems

In the first period, most patients deny having any problems. Their eating disorder is not a problem for them, but a *solution* to the problems they had before they started to diet. Their motivation to start dieting was not only to lose weight, but also to acquire more self-esteem and feel more positive about themselves and their body. When they start a diet, they feel that they have control over their food and feel very proud of their slimming behaviour. The first stage of dieting increases their self-esteem and improves their self-image. At that stage, they do not experience any problems; on the contrary, their eating habits are seen as an important solution to all kinds of problems they had. Before they started their extreme dieting, they felt they had no control over their lives, had a very negative self-evaluation and lack of self-esteem and had many negative emotions, but dieting gave them a strong feeling of control, developed self-esteem and reduced and suppressed all the negative emotions. These effects of the first stage of extreme dieting were seen as very positive. So why give up?

Extreme dieting gives patients so many positive experiences that they are not at all motivated to change their eating habits. On the contrary, they want to continue their dieting regime in order to have control over their body. They are proud of their successful strategy of food reduction and weight loss and are able to suppress their negative feelings and emotions. At that stage, they are not at all motivated to change their eating habits.

It is not until much later, when they are confronted with all kinds of unexpected negative physical, psychological and social consequences, that they realize that their eating habits not only offer positive experiences but also have many negative consequences. But even then, they feel their eating habits are rewarding, because they feel in control of their life, which motivates them to continue their extreme dieting.

Summary

This chapter was about the first stage of dieting and losing weight, which patients see as very positive because it gives them self-esteem and control. Slimming behaviour is experienced as a *solution* to all their problems, such as low self-esteem and negative body image. Extreme dieting functions as a way of coping with these problems. Patients' feelings of self-esteem and control over their body increase, and this first positive evaluation of their dieting motivates them to continue at an extreme level. Only when they are confronted with all kinds of negative physical, psychological and social problems do they realize that their extreme dieting does not bring what they hoped for. The negative consequences will be described in Chapter 3.

3

Negative Consequences of Eating Disorders

Introduction

In this chapter, the negative psychological, social and physical consequences of eating disorders are described. Patients become obsessed with food and weight and develop all kinds of rigid rules; their cognition about food and weight is quite disturbed. Although they experienced the first stage of their extreme dieting as highly positive and welcomed the eating disorder as a friend, they finally realize that their disorder is akin to an enemy that destroys their lives. Many eating disorder patients are no longer able to continue their education or job and become more and more isolated. They suffer from all kinds of physical complaints. When the negative consequences become very serious and dominate their lives, they realize that the eating disorder has become a trap from which it is difficult to escape.

Losing Control over Eating Habits

Extreme dieting and losing weight give strong feelings of power and control. According to Bruch (1978), control over eating habits gives patients, for the first time in their lives, the feeling that their personality has a core and that they are connected with their feelings. Therefore, they want to continue their eating habits even when they are confronted with many negative consequences. They are afraid that they might lose their feeling of identity and control if they were to gain weight.

Recovery from Eating Disorders: A Guide for Clinicians and Their Clients,
First Edition. Greta Noordenbos.

It is striking that anorectic patients are unable to see how emaciated their body has become. The prouder they are of their extreme slimming behaviour, the less they see how skeletally thin their body has become. According to Bruch (1978), their self-deceit protects them from a fundamental feeling of desperation, with their slimming behaviour as the only foothold that gives them a feeling of identity and control.

> LISETTE: 'The idea that I should stop dieting made me panic. I was afraid that my feeling of "self" might disintegrate into nothing and nobody. If somebody had forced me to be fed and to gain weight I might have committed suicide, because my fear of losing my feeling of identity and disappearing as a person was extremely high.'

The more they starve themselves, the more they become obsessed with food. Some anorectic patients become interested in cooking for others, but not for themselves. They even dream about food. Extreme restriction of food intake increases the risk that they are no longer able to control their food intake and begin to develop small *binges*, which eventually become bigger, real binges.

> ANITA: 'When I had anorexia, I felt awful, but I still had the illusion I had control over my body. When I discovered that I was able to vomit at will, nothing could stop me any more. I became completely addicted to food and several times a day I had a binge. Finally I realized that I had completely lost all control of my eating behaviour.'

A binge is often preceded by feelings of negative emotions and stress and functions as a way to get rid of these unbearable feelings. During a binge, the patient eats large amounts of food, which is swallowed without tasting and chewing. Because of their fear of gaining weight after a binge, they try to get rid of the food in their stomach as soon as possible by self-induced vomiting, laxatives or extreme exercising. When frequent binges are followed by compensating behaviour, patients can be diagnosed as having bulimia nervosa. Not all people who have binges, however, compensate or purge afterwards. In such cases, we speak about a binge eating disorder (BED). Having binges without compensating behaviour results in weight increase, often leading to obesity.

The transformation from anorectic to bulimic behaviour is described as a process of *crossover* which is often found in eating disorder patients. Therefore, Fairburn, Cooper, and Shafran (2003) developed a transdiagnostic approach in diagnosing and treating eating disorder patients.

The Trap of Extreme Dieting

The first period of dieting and weight loss is very rewarding and gives patients the feeling that they have found the ultimate *solution* for their lack of self-esteem and control. However, what started as a positive experience to increase self-esteem sooner or later turns out to be a trap. The feeling of control is only related to eating and weight, while patients' psychosocial development stagnates. When they are confronted with the negative consequences, they slowly realize that their *solution* is no effective strategy for their problems. At that stage, however, it is very difficult for them to stop their extreme dieting, because of their fear of losing their self-esteem, identity and feeling of control.

Some patients report that the eating disorder dominates their lives completely. The disorder becomes a trap or prison from which they cannot escape. Bruch (1978) sees anorexia nervosa as an *astray* in the development of independence and a form of fundamental self-deception.

Some bulimic patients get completely caught up in the compulsive binging and purging behaviour which dominates their entire lives. Their first experience of dieting as a solution for their problems turns out to be a trap. At that moment, however, they are unable to get out of it.

TINA: 'I knew that I damaged my body but I did not know any other way to keep myself going. I was absolutely unable to change my behaviour. I really had become a prisoner of my eating disorder.'

RUBY: 'My extreme slimming behaviour was the only positive aspect in my life which was really a bit of me. If I stopped my slimming behaviour I might lose all feeling of existing as a person and lose my whole identity. It felt as if my feelings of having a "self" would fall apart and sink into a deep sea.'

Eating Disorder: From Friend to Enemy

During the first stage, an eating disorder is often considered a friend who provides a feeling of control. In the following letter, Carmen sees her eating disorder as a *friend*.

CARMEN: 'Dear binges you are the most important experiences in my life. You are my support and my anchor. All other things become irrelevant when I see what you do for me. When I have a binge I do not feel isolated, and when I am in deep despair, for the moment you give me the pleasurable feeling that I may eat everything I want...' (Spaans & Bloks, 2008, p. 138).

At a later stage, however, patients are confronted with all kinds of negative consequences and find that the eating disorder does not bring what they hoped for. The disorder is no longer a friend but becomes an enemy (Tierney & Fox, 2010). This is clearly described by Isabel in her letter referring to her anorexia as an enemy:

ISABEL: 'I hate you. You never leave me alone. I can never eat in peace. If I want to eat with friends you start to nag: Why do you want to eat that? It is better not to eat that. Then you spoil everything.'

NATASCHA WRITES IN HER DIARY (2006): 'I do not exactly know when he came into my life. Suddenly he was there. A friend, I thought. But more and more I came to the conclusion that he was no friend at all. He forbade me to enjoy my life. He was scolding and insulting me. And I listened to him, and his name was Anorexia Nervosa.'

It took Natascha a long time to discover that she felt profoundly betrayed by what she thought was a friend:

NATASCHA: 'Dear Anorexia. What do you want from me? You say that you are a friend and will always guarantee my safety. You say that I can always trust you and you are there for me, even when the world is cold and dangerous. But do I want you to always order me about? Because that is what you do. You punish me when I cannot fulfil your high expectations. I really feel not well, even quite bad, even worse than before to tell you the truth. You try to break me and make me addicted to slimming, even when it becomes dangerous.'

These experiences make it clear that an eating disorder is not a friend at all. A real friend is a person who visits you, is interested in your well-being and comforts you when you feel bad. A real friend is one who will phone you and invite you over to discuss issues that are important to you. When necessary, a friend confronts you with your failings and misapprehensions. You can laugh and cry with a real friend, but with an eating disorder you cannot laugh at all; on the contrary, all pleasure disappears from your life. Sooner or later you become isolated and depressed because of the negative consequences of your eating disorder.

Rigid Rules and Obsessive-Compulsive Behaviour

Eating disorder patients develop all kinds of obsessive thoughts and behaviour. Anorectic patients become obsessed by the amount of calories they think they are allowed to eat. They look carefully at the number of calories in everything they eat and count how many calories they have already consumed and how much they are likely to consume during their next meal. They are also always calculating the number of calories they have burned by extreme exercising.

> MIRJAM: 'I developed all kinds of rules about places and times to eat. That gave me a feeling of control. Breaking these rules and rigid schedules felt as a complete loss of control.'

It is not only anorectic patients but bulimic patients as well who develop all kinds of rituals and obsessive-compulsive behaviour.

> PETRA: 'Each binge felt as extreme loss of control over my eating behaviour, and I tried to get rid of the food in my stomach as soon as possible by vomiting, by using laxatives or by extreme exercising.'

Binges are often followed by all kinds of rules aimed at *cleaning* the body, which has to be *purified*. Purging, however, makes the stomach empty, thereby triggering the next binge. Some bulimic patients not only feel the need to purify their stomach and bowels, but also feel the urge to purify their body by washing their hands frequently and taking showers several times a day.

> CAROL: 'I had developed all kinds of obsessive behaviour by doing exercises, jogging etcetera. I became completely involved in obsessive-compulsive rituals and took often showers for a long time. I no longer had time for other activities.'

When they break their strict rules, they feel they have lost control over their lives. According to Bruch (1978), anorectic girls treat themselves like convicts who are not allowed any comfort and only get minimum food while being forced to labour continuously until they are completely exhausted. They keep themselves on a tight rein and often feel the need to punish themselves when they eat more than allowed. They do not allow themselves to do anything for their own pleasure.

Indoctrination and Brainwashing

Patients who develop anorexia nervosa frequently repeat the following dogmas: 'eating less is better and eating more is bad' and 'losing weight is positive and gaining weight negative.' Over and over they repeat: 'To consume calories is bad because calories make you fat.'

They are comparable to people who have been brainwashed and indoctrinated. These concepts are rarely used in the case of eating disorders, because most people associate brainwashing and indoctrination with politics or religious ideas. But for eating disorder patients, these concepts seem to be very apt, as described by Hilde Bruch (1978). They brainwash themselves to prevent weight gain: their feelings of hunger are felt as positive and safe and they are proud of being able to resist hunger, which gives them a feeling of control and self-esteem. Some of them even develop feelings of superiority when they compare themselves with others who are not able to continue their diet.

> MARCEL: 'I can resist food, while other people who are "weak" have to admit that they need food.'
> ANOTHER PATIENT OF BRUCH (1978, pp. 86/87) says: 'You brainwash yourself – and once you start on that path, then you become blind to what is going on.'

Pro-Ana web sites, in which anorectic patients stimulate each other to become as thin as possible, are clear examples of indoctrination. These sites advocate a destructive way of thinking, and anorectic behaviour is promoted as a *style of living*. The dogmas about slimming behaviour are seen as irrefutable. Reactions to people who are not able to lose weight are extremely negative and denigrating. Pro-Ana sites are very dangerous because they stimulate patients to continue their unhealthy eating habits. Therefore, it is important to protect victims against indoctrination by extreme dogmas about weight loss in pro-Ana sites.

Inner Criticism and Critical Voices

Eating disorder patients often have very negative and critical thoughts about themselves. Although at first the dieting successes give them positive feelings, these feelings may sooner or later evaporate, while the negative and critical thoughts increase.

> WENDY: 'I was always very negative about myself and extremely critical, even when I did succeed to eat less and to lose weight. When I ate only a little more than my strict diet allowed I had to compensate for that, and to eat less during the rest of the day. I was very critical of my food intake and weight, but also of other aspects of my behaviour. When I could not meet the high standards I had set for myself I scolded myself: "you always make mistakes, you can never do anything right, you are stupid, you are a loser", etcetera.'

After a binge, bulimic patients often have very negative thoughts about themselves.

GWEN: 'When I was unable to control my food intake any longer and started to have binges I hated myself. I became really sick of myself. I forced myself to vomit, although that was a terrible and painful experience. But I had to punish myself and forced myself to go running for hours, until I was completely exhausted. Then I tried to sleep and forget the bad experience.'

These negative and critical thoughts are described by psychologists as 'inner criticism' (Sterk & Swaen, 2006), 'inner negativism' (Claude-Pierre, 1997) or 'inner saboteur' (Kortink, 2008). Negative thoughts can dominate eating disorder patients' lives, as becomes clear from Ann's experiences:

ANN: 'I was completely overwhelmed by all the negative thoughts which completely undermined my self-respect. Nothing was good enough, everything I did I could have done better.'

At the serious stage of their eating disorder, some patients hear a negative *voice* in their heads (Bruch, 1978; Noordenbos, Boesenach, Moerman, & Trommelen, 2012; Tierney & Fox, 2010).

BEA: 'When I had severe anorexia nervosa I continually heard that voice in my head which always criticized me. It was like the voice of an inner dictator. After each small bit of food I heard the voice saying: "that was wrong, you were not allowed to eat that, now you have to be punished, and you are not allowed to eat the rest of the day, because you already ate too much". It was terrible to hear that voice, but I was unable to resist it. This continuous critical voice in my head made me very powerless.'

How to explain the development of hearing disapproving inner voices? A possible explanation might be that eating disorder patients start to develop very strict rules about their food intake, which function as their inner conscience or superego. The more extreme their diet and the more undernourished their body, the less they are able to resist their inner critical thoughts, which are heard as a voice in the head (Heffner & Eifert, 2004).

NATASCHA: 'I was no longer able to go to school and was allowed to eat only one apple a day. But even when I ate that apple I had to punish myself because of the calories and sugar in the apple, which was not allowed.'

Anorectic patients have a very strict superego, which suppresses their biological needs and desires. They are completely ruled by their superego, which can be compared to a dictator who does not allow them to have any pleasure or satisfaction in life.

NATASCHA: 'After some time I no longer had any feelings of pleasure. My willpower was very strong and my whole life was aimed at high achievements in studies and dieting.'

Some eating disorder patients report that they were completely dominated by their inner *monster*. They had to obey very stringent rules and felt bad or guilty when they could not meet those rules. They were not able to ignore the strict rules of their superego and were not allowed to do things for their own pleasure. They completely neglected their own physical needs. Hilde Bruch (1978, p. 9) described that some anorectic patients experience an *inner dictator* in their mind who forbids them to satisfy their physical needs and forces them to refuse food.

The inner voice functions as an overbearing superego, which completely dominates them and prevents them from eating healthy amounts of food. This becomes clear in the following struggle of Mara with her inner voice (Nottelman & Thijsen, 2010).

MARA: 'After I ate some crisps I had the following conversation in my head:

"*How dare you. You are a weakling! You ate forbidden food. Crisps, even. You have to throw that out. Vomit, now!*"

But I do not want to vomit any more. I have not vomited for three weeks now; I really want to stop throwing up.

But do you want to keep that awful stuff in your body? Impossible, you have to throw it up.

But to eat crisps is not so bad, is it? It might be a snack, but it's not very unhealthy.

Do you really think that this makes no difference? Of course, it will affect your body weight. You ate CRISPS. That is forbidden. And now they are in your dirty fat stomach. So hurry up and throw it out.
Reluctantly I go to the toilet to throw up. But I do not want to throw up. Why am I doing this?

So hurry up. The longer that stuff is inside you, the more it will be absorbed in your body.

I put a finger in my throat, but I can't vomit. I am drinking some more luke-warm water and again trying to throw up. But I can't, I will stop.

No way, even when you get a sore throat you NEED to get that stuff out of your body.

Finally I threw up half of the crisps I had in my stomach and started to cry.'

In her book, Mara makes it very clear how much of an impact this inner voice has on her, and how difficult it is for her to resist the negative voice.

Research by Noordenbos et al. (2012) shows that hearing a negative inner voice mostly starts at the beginning of the eating disorder and becomes more dominant at the later, serious stage of the disorder. The more strict and dominant the inner voice, the less patients are able to resist it.

RUBEN: 'It is as of you have become a robot and are no longer able to decide for yourself what you want.'

JOAN: 'I had the feeling as if a slave driver forced me to do all kinds of activities which exhausted me.'

Their entire existence has become a struggle against their inner dictator.

The Toxic Effects of Starvation

Patients with anorexia nervosa, as well as bulimic patients with extreme purging behaviour, suffer from all kinds of consequences of starvation. Bruch (1978) describes how starvation can severely disturb the mental and emotional state of patients. Sensorial perception can become more extreme, resulting in hallucinogenic experiences in some patients. These hallucinations also figure in the experiences of saints in the past, who had visions after a period of extreme fasting (Vandereycken & van Deth, 1994).

At the stage of severe starvation, all personal characteristics disappear, and eating disorder patients become more and more alike in appearance, emotions, thoughts and behaviour. Bruch (1978) speaks about the *toxic* effects of malnutrition and starvation. At the starvation stage, patients are no longer able to experience emotions and lose all contact with reality.

ISABEL: 'I became very numb and it felt as if I did not really exist any more. I was no longer able to communicate with other people and nothing interested me any more. I had the feeling that people were not able to understand my way of thinking and feeling. It was as if my body was poisoned, as if I was permanently drunk or stoned.'

ANGELA: 'My thoughts became very unrealistic. I had the feeling that I had to obey a strong voice in my head which controlled my whole life. I was completely outside myself. My body became the visual symbol of pure ascetic and aesthetic values and no critical comments could reach me.'

At this critical stage, some eating disorder patients often dissociate between body and mind.

JEANET: 'I remember that at a certain moment I was no longer in my body, and was watching my body from outside. It was as if I was looking at a film, as if I walked beside my body and was no longer inside it.'

ESTHER: 'Everything became very intense and spiritual, but completely unrealistic. Starvation had the same impact as using drugs, and I had no longer any contact with my body I was completely dissociated from it. It was as if I had developed a different level of consciousness. The consequence of starvation was that I no longer felt any pain. This was a kind of self-hypnosis.'

In the long run, severely emaciated patients can lose all feeling of time and reality.

BEA: 'Losing all consciousness of time was amazing. It was as if time went very fast, but on the other hand the days seemed extremely long.'

According to Bruch (1978), severe weight loss and starvation lead to a toxic situation in which the patients develop a different state of consciousness and abnormal ideas about their food intake and body. Because of the severe physical and psychological consequences of starvation, such as dissociation from the body, depersonalization and feelings of numbness, psychotherapy is very difficult at this stage. Patients are no longer able to reflect on their own behaviour, thoughts and emotions. Their way of thinking is severely disorganized, and they are no longer able to think logically about food and weight. Starvation also has consequences for the neurological and hormonal system and can even lead to reduced brain volume (Keel, 2005).

Depression and Suicidal Thoughts

The most frequent psychological consequences of undernourishment are an obsession with food and weight, lack of concentration, restlessness and hyperactivity (Elburg, 2007a). Sooner or later patients become depressed and lose all interest in life.

Although patients start their extreme dieting to develop more self-esteem, in the end they become very negative about themselves and all positive feelings fade away. Instead of feeling better, they feel extremely sad and no longer experience any positive emotions. Everything becomes grey and sad.

ULRIKE: 'At the last, critical stage of my eating disorder everything I did was exhausting. I did not feel any emotions and was no longer able to laugh or to cry.'
SUZANNE: 'When I was so emaciated I no longer had any sexual feelings. All pleasure was gone and everything was painful. I was hurting all over my body.'

At the most critical stage of the eating disorder, all positive effects of the first stage vanish and only negative and depressive feelings remain.

Sometimes, patients become suicidal and long for death. Their body is severely damaged and nothing in their life is worthwhile any more.

> CAROLINE: 'I became severely depressed. Although I did go to school nothing interested me any more. I felt tired and completely exhausted. During that critical stage of my eating disorder I was hardly alive. I really cannot remember that period, because all days seemed to be the same grey colour. I mostly lay in bed and often wished that I might not wake up the next morning.'

When all feelings of pleasure disappear from their lives, they become seriously depressed and suicidal.

> WILLIAM: 'I was very depressed and deep within me I hoped that a car would hit me so that I would die and no longer had to go on living.'

Some patients have outspoken suicidal thoughts and want to end their life.

> BIANCA: 'I was very afraid of being alone, because of the delusions I had. I really was afraid that I would kill myself, because I wished I would not have to live any longer.'
> GRACE: 'I really wanted to be dead. I felt like a wreck. I was completely addicted to valium and felt utterly broken.'
> HILDE: 'In that critical period I was preparing for suicide because I was unable to continue to live in that way.'

Questionnaire about psychological consequences

Do you have the following psychological problems?

You can answer 1=no, 2=a little, 3=somewhat, 4=yes, 5=very much

1.	I am obsessed by food and weight	1	2	3	4	5
2.	I have rigid rules about my food intake	1	2	3	4	5
3.	I punish myself if I break these rules	1	2	3	4	5
4.	I suffer from obsessive-compulsive behaviour	1	2	3	4	5
5.	I often criticize myself after food intake	1	2	3	4	5
6.	I have critical thoughts about my weight	1	2	3	4	5
7.	I am afraid of losing control over my food intake	1	2	3	4	5
8.	I often lose control over my food intake	1	2	3	4	5
9.	I have very critical thoughts about myself	1	2	3	4	5
10.	I hear inner critical voices	1	2	3	4	5
11.	I often struggle with my inner critical voice	1	2	3	4	5
12.	I have hallucinogenic experiences	1	2	3	4	5

13. I feel disconnected with my body	1	2	3	4	5
14. I have unrealistic thoughts and experiences	1	2	3	4	5
15. I feel very sad and down	1	2	3	4	5
16. I feel depressed	1	2	3	4	5
17. I have suicidal thoughts	1	2	3	4	5

Other psychological problems:

18.	1	2	3	4	5
19.	1	2	3	4	5
20.	1	2	3	4	5

You can discuss your answers with your therapist. Questions which you have answered with 3, 4 or 5 are important to be addressed in your treatment.

Isolation

An important motivation for going on a diet is the hope to gain more friends and to become more accepted. At the first stage of an eating disorder, the social consequences are not yet apparent, because patients often have a *double life* in which they behave normally with others and try to hide their distorted eating habits as much as possible. They avoid contact with others because they are afraid that they may discover how disturbed their eating habits are and urge them to eat more. However, in the long run the social consequences of their eating disorder become more serious. They distrust others, lose friends and are unable to continue their education or job. Sooner or later, eating disorder patients lose contact with other people. The longer they have the eating disorder, the more isolated they become and the more they lock themselves from society (Bruch, 1978).

ESTHER: 'Instead of being more accepted by others I was often involved in arguments. My father would become very angry and beat his fist on the table, shouting: eat! My mother often started to cry. Sometimes my father did not speak to me for days. The situation at home became unbearable.'

KIRSTIN: 'I slowly realized that something went wrong. I stayed in bed until late in the morning. Because of my binging and vomiting late in the evening I felt physically awful. In the end I lost all contact with my friends and never went out.'

THALIA: 'In the most critical period of my eating disorder social contacts did not interest me any more and I never went out to see other people, because I was very afraid that I would be made to eat. At that critical stage of my eating disorder I spent most of the time alone in my room.'

CATHY: 'I felt more and more desperate. Each night I had binges, and in the morning I felt very bad and had a headache. I took many laxatives and often was not able to go to my job. But staying at home made my situation even worse, because at home there was nothing to distract me from binging and purging. The whole day I was thinking about food and vomiting, and all my energy was gone so that I was unable to get out of bed. I only got out of bed to have a binge and to vomit. Afterwards I was exhausted and had to sleep. Eventually I slept on the couch in the living room with a large bucket beside me which I could use as a toilet.'

At the critical stage, contacts with other people become reduced and the social world grows very small.

Questionnaire about social consequences

Do you have the following social problems?

You can answer 1=no, 2=a little, 3=somewhat, 4=yes, 5=very much

1.	I feel isolated	1	2	3	4	5
2.	I have few social activities	1	2	3	4	5
3.	I find it difficult to initiate contacts with others	1	2	3	4	5
4.	I do not have close friends	1	2	3	4	5
5.	I do not dare to talk about personal experiences	1	2	3	4	5
6.	I have problems in the contact with my parents	1	2	3	4	5
7.	I am not able to continue my education	1	2	3	4	5
8.	I am not able to study	1	2	3	4	5
9.	I am not able to continue my job	1	2	3	4	5

Other social problems:

10.	....	1	2	3	4	5
11.	....	1	2	3	4	5
12.	....	1	2	3	4	5

You can discuss your answers with your therapist. Questions which you have answered with 3, 4 or 5 are important to be addressed in your treatment.

Physical Consequences

Extreme dieting has all kinds of negative physical consequences, such as tiredness, lack of energy, low temperature, brittle nails, damage to teeth, constipation, stomach and bowel problems, low heartbeat, disturbed sleep, and so on. In case of severe emaciation, the body feels exhausted and very painful. When all fat tissue has disappeared, patients sit directly on their bones, because the skin has become very thin. They cannot sleep because they feel hungry and constantly think about food. Some others cannot sleep because lying in bed becomes very painful in their emaciated state. Many anorectic patients become very restless and hyperactive when their body urgently needs food (Elburg, 2007a).

The comments from the following patients make it clear how much they have suffered from the physical consequences of their eating disorder.

KATHY: 'I always felt very tired and my whole body was painful. When I lay in bed, I clearly felt my bones because I had no fat left under my skin. Moreover, I had many painful places on my skin because it had become very thin.'

MIRIAM: 'I constantly had this painful feeling of hunger. Sometimes I was trembling because my job as a nurse was quite demanding. In those situations I took a little sugar, because otherwise I ran the risk of fainting.'

HENRY: 'Because of extreme dieting I lost much weight, but I also lost my energy and felt extremely tired. My body temperature was very low, and I was always cold, even in summer.'

ANN: 'After severe emaciation I had no fat left between my skin and my bones, which was very painful. My hair fell out and my skin became very dry. Because of the frequent vomiting the enamel of my teeth had become very thin, so that drinking hot tea or cold water was very painful. The condition of my teeth was very bad. Each time I was brushing my teeth my gums started to bleed.'

These quotes show that eating disorders have very damaging effects on the body. Because of the lack of food and extreme emaciation, the production of hormones decreases for both women and men (Keel, 2005). Female anorectic patients have irregular periods or no menses at all. Many patients develop osteoporosis. Some have heart problems, because of a lack of calcium as a consequence of vomiting and frequent use of laxatives. When their physical condition deteriorates, patients start to worry about their health.

RACHEL: 'There came a point in my life when I could see that my body was very emaciated, and I got scared of that. My bones were clearly visible and when I was sunbathing my hips became easily sunburned, which was very painful.'

KAREN: 'When I started to vomit blood I became very scared about my health.'

LISETTE: 'Eventually I was no longer able to sleep. At three o'clock in the morning I went to the kitchen, to get some food from the refrigerator, so that the pain in my stomach would disappear. For many years I slept only a few hours during the night.'

Some eating disorder patients become addicted to alcohol or valium in order to reduce their feelings of tension and stress.

SOPHIE: 'When I was alone I started to drink alcohol, and because I ate hardly anything a little alcohol was enough to send me to sleep. Alcohol helped me to continue my dieting behaviour, but also had many negative consequences. My face became swollen, as did my fingers and feet. In order to reduce that I took diuretics and laxatives, but that made me sink even deeper into the pit of my eating disorder.'

JESSICA: 'In the end I was completely addicted to valium. I got oedema and had severe problems with my kidneys. But I did not dare to complain about that, because I was afraid that my parents would send me to the doctor. Eventually my hair fell out and I could no longer hide the physical consequences of my eating disorder from others.'

Questionnaire about physical consequences

Do you have the following physical problems?

You can answer 1=no, 2=a little, 3=somewhat, 4=yes, 5=very much

1a.	My weight is very low	1	2	3	4	5?
1b.	My weight is very high	1	2	3	4	5
2.	My weight is unstable	1	2	3	4	5
3.	My periods are irregular	1	2	3	4	5
4.	I have had no periods in three months	1	2	3	4	5
5.	My body temperature is low	1	2	3	4	5
6.	My heart rate is low	1	2	3	4	5
7a.	My blood pressure is low	1	2	3	4	5
7b.	My blood pressure is high	1	2	3	4	5
8.	I have constipation	1	2	3	4	5
9.	I have bowel problems	1	2	3	4	5
10.	I have stomach problems	1	2	3	4	5
11.	My skin is dry	1	2	3	4	5
12.	My teeth are damaged	1	2	3	4	5
13.	My gums often bleed	1	2	3	4	5
14.	I do not get enough sleep	1	2	3	4	5
15.	My sleeping pattern is disturbed	1	2	3	4	5
16.	I often feel very tired	1	2	3	4	5
17.	I often feel exhausted	1	2	3	4	5

Other physical problems:

18.	....	1	2	3	4	5
19.	....	1	2	3	4	5
20.	....	1	2	3	4	5

You can discuss your answers with your therapist. The questions to which you have answered 3, 4 or 5 are especially important to address in your treatment.

Summary

In this chapter, all kinds of negative physical, psychological and social consequences of an eating disorder were described. The chapter also described patients' obsession with food and weight and their apprehension of gaining weight. Eating disorder patients become very isolated and are no longer able to continue with their education or job. They become severely emaciated and exhausted, their body temperature is reduced and they often have stomach and bowel problems. When the negative consequences become very grave and dominate their lives, they realize that this is not what they had hoped for. They have hit the bottom of the pit. This desperate feeling may lead to a turning point after which they become motivated to recover, as will be described in Chapter 4.

4

Turning Point and Motivation for Recovery

Introduction

At the first stage of dieting, eating disorder patients deny having any problems. On the contrary, they see their dieting as a positive thing because it gives them a feeling of self-esteem, identity and control. These positive feelings motivate them to continue their diet in a more extreme way. The first stage of dieting is not felt as a problem but as a solution to all the various problems they have. Therefore, at this point they are not at all motivated to change their eating habits. They have found an important strategy to improve their self-esteem and body image and feel in control of their life. Extreme dieting helps them to reduce their negative emotions and stress.

However extreme dieting only works as a solution for a short period, because this strategy has many negative physical, psychological and social consequences. When these negative consequences completely dominate patients' lives, they become convinced that they cannot continue their eating habits. But even when they realize that the eating disorder has life-threatening consequences, their motivation to change is still ambivalent. Although they want to recover from the negative consequences of their eating disorder, they are afraid of gaining weight and of losing their self-respect, identity and control.

Although most motivating strategies for eating disorder patients are directed at improving their food intake and weight (Bloks & Spaans, 2008), this is actually felt as very frightening and threatening. A better strategy is to motivate them by focusing on reducing the negative physical consequences and on improving their self-esteem, body attitude and coping strategies.

Recovery from Eating Disorders: A Guide for Clinicians and Their Clients,
First Edition. Greta Noordenbos.
© 2013 John Wiley & Sons, Ltd. Published 2013 by John Wiley & Sons, Ltd.

Several questionnaires can be filled in order to find what motivates eating disorder patients to improve and recover.

The Deep Pit

In the long run, eating disorder patients feel that they have sunk into a deep pit or swamp and are unable to climb out of it. The first positive experiences of increased self-esteem and control disappear completely, and the eating disorder becomes a prison from which they cannot escape.

> DORITH: 'In the first period of my slimming behaviour I felt very good: I was very successful at losing weight, which was really great. But the more weight I lost, the more depressed I felt. I was also very tired and weary. I did not feel emotions any more and all days were sad and boring. It felt as if I had fallen into a deep pit and I did not know how to get out of it. When I started dieting I hoped to feel better and more happy, but the result was that I became extremely unhappy and depressed.'

Also bulimic patients realize that having binges is not the solution for their feelings of stress but produces even more problems. This is clearly described in Olaf's account of his experiences:

> OLAF: 'I often became upset when colleagues made negative comments on my behaviour. I tried to avoid them, but their remarks stayed in my mind. The tension increased if I was unable to finish all activities I had planned for that day. That made me see myself in a very negative light. I always felt I was failing. When I came home I felt so completely stressed that the first thing I did was to go to the kitchen and eat everything I could find in the refrigerator. I just crammed all the food into my mouth and swallowed everything that was available: bread, pudding, cheese, yoghurt, everything. When at last I felt full and exhausted, I realised what I had done and tried to get rid of all that food by drinking some glasses of water and vomiting as soon as possible. After vomiting I felt very tired and I lay down on the couch. In the evening I was no longer able to do anything, I did not visit friends or go out to do some sport. If the phone rang I did not answer. Each day I wanted to change my behaviour and stop having binges followed by purging, but each day I urgently needed a binge when I came home from my job. That went on for months and I became more and more isolated and depressed.'

When patients start to use many laxatives, their physical condition deteriorates, as becomes clear from the following account:

BIANCA: 'To prevent weight gain I often took some laxatives before eating a slice of bread or a sandwich. Those laxatives filled my stomach and reduced my feelings of hunger. Moreover, when I ate my bread they made the food run through my intestines very quickly so that there was no time to absorb the calories. This strategy, however, had grave consequences. I often had considerable pain in my stomach and urgently needed to go to the toilet. My intestines had to work very hard which caused cramps and terrible pain. After several months I was no longer able to go to school, although my school performance was very important to me. I finally decided to take fewer laxatives, but then my stomach felt hugely swollen because of constipation. My intestines had become inactive and if I did not take laxatives I could not go to the toilet. This situation went on for more than a year before I realized that I was ruining my body. All day long I was busy with food, laxatives and sitting on the toilet, to the exclusion of everything else. I desperately wanted to go to school, but felt too tired. I really wanted to change my life and to get rid of these laxatives and the pain in my stomach.'

The most critical stage of the eating disorder can be compared to driving a car which has gotten stuck in the mud. When the driver presses the accelerator to come out of the mud, the car gets more entrenched.

JOHAN: 'I started dieting in order to lose weight and hoped that people would like me better. But after a first positive period all kinds of negative physical consequences became noticeable: I always felt tired and my temperature became very low so that I always had cold hands and feet. I was no longer able to swim because the water was too cold for me. My body temperature was very low. At home I was always sitting next to the central heating. I slept very badly because I was always hungry and my whole body hurt, even when I lay in a soft bed. I lost my concentration in school. Finally I realized that the extreme restriction of calorie intake did not bring me what I longed for. I did not have any pleasure in my life and all days felt grey and sad. Life could not get much worse: I really wanted to find a way out of this dreadful situation.'

Turning Point

When the negative consequences become very serious, eating disorder patients realize that they cannot continue their way of life. They feel completely locked up in the prison of their eating disorder. They have hit the bottom of the pit and have sunk deep into the swamp. They realize that by continuing their eating habits, they risk death. At this stage, many eating disorder patients experience a *turning point*, when they feel that they need to change. Some patients realize that they have to choose between life and death.

JENNY: 'Because of the laxatives I used after each binge I had many problems with my bowels, which did not work any more. Therefore, I needed to take many laxatives, but the more laxatives I used, the more my stomach hurt. Sometimes the pain was so extreme that I was sitting on the toilet for hours and had the feeling that my intestines were coming out of my body, which was extremely painful. Then I realized that I could not continue any longer and I needed help in order to change my life.'

ADINA: 'At the most severe stage of my eating disorder I was not capable of anything except lying in bed, but even that was very painful because my skin had become very thin and I always felt my bones. I was extremely depressed and lost all pleasure in life. I felt that my body was completely exhausted and that I might die. Then I realized that I actually could choose whether to live or to die. And at that moment I chose to live. That was an important turning point in my life.'

RUTH: 'I only became motivated for treatment when I could no longer go to school and became very isolated. The only contacts I had were with my parents and my sister. But even these contacts were not satisfying, because we always quarreled about my food and weight. My dad became very angry and my mother often cried. My sister often went to her friends because she could not handle the situation at home. I felt very depressed and often stayed in my room, where I tried to read and watch television. But even reading books was no longer possible because I could not concentrate any more. Then I realised that this was absolutely not what I had wanted. My life could not become much worse. Then I was convinced that I had to change in order to survive.'

BEA: 'I think that it was extremely difficult to help me and to change my eating behaviour, until I reached the limit of my physical existence. Before that point I was not motivated to change.'

Some eating disorder patients who intended to commit suicide realized that another choice was possible:

TALITHA: 'Only after five years of having an eating disorder did I realize that I was not able to continue my life in that way. My weight had become extreme low and I wanted to stop. But then I discovered that I was no longer able to stop my anorectic way of thinking and to eat more. Each time when I ate a slice of bread I had to take ten laxatives. I had many physical problems such as oedema and problems with my kidneys, but even then I could not stop. That was a shocking experience, because I always thought that I had control over my food intake. But it was the anorexia which controlled my life. So I finally realized that I needed help, or I would die.'

Sooner or later most eating disorder patients realize that their eating habits impede their physical, psychological and social functioning. The quality of life deteriorates, bordering on death, and they feel they can no longer continue their way of life. Many patients experience a turning point when they realize that they need to change in order to improve their physical, psychological and social well-being. It is then that they slowly become motivated to change and to find help. However, their motivation to change is highly ambivalent, because they fear losing their self-esteem and control over their lives.

Ambivalent Motivation for Change

Although many eating disorder patients experience a turning point when they become motivated to change, this motivation is often very ambivalent. They are afraid of losing control over their food intake and gaining weight and are critical of themselves when they eat more than they think they should. For some eating disorder patients, it feels as if they might have to give up their way of life and lose their identity. Moreover, suffering from an eating disorder for a long time means that feelings of hunger and satiety become disturbed. Serotonin and hormone production become severely impaired. Their body has become accustomed to their way of eating. Their brain can also be affected, and in case of severe starvation there is a decrease in brain volume (Keel, 2005). Because of these serious physical, neurological and psychological consequences, it is not easy for patients to change, even when they experience a turning point and become motivated to change and to recover.

Although most eating disorder patients admit that their disorder has many negative consequences, there is a great fear to change, which makes it very difficult for them to become motivated for change and treatment. There is a huge gap between their recognizing that they have an eating problem and becoming motivated to change.

> BIONDA: 'I think that when you have anorexia nervosa it is very difficult to become motivated to change. The problem is that you know you will lose something and you do not know what you will gain afterwards. You also have to admit that all those years you spent having this eating behaviour have brought no real solution for your problems. That is very painful. You not only have to give up your eating behaviour and control, but your whole identity and way of living have to change. All day long I was thinking about food and weight and without that I felt I was nobody. That was very frightening.'

Although eating disorder patients suffer from all kinds of negative physical, psychological and social consequences, they find it very difficult to change their eating habits, because they are afraid of losing their self-esteem and control over their lives. They are scared that all the problems they had before the eating disorder may return, such as low self-esteem, negative body image and inability to express their emotions and needs.

ANGELA: 'I really want to improve, but then I will have to eat more and gain weight, and I am very scared of that.'

PETER: 'Yes, I am motivated to improve the quality of my life but that implies that I have to abandon control over my food and I will lose the anchor in my life.'

GRACE: 'I want to get rid of all the physical consequences of my eating disorder, but then I will also lose my feeling of identity, because the eating disorder has become such an important part of myself.'

HELENA: 'I only became motivated to change my eating behaviour when there were so many negative physical consequences that the quality of my life had become very low. I could not sleep any more because of the hunger pains, and my whole body hurt because I had no fat under my skin. Because of lack of sleep I was no longer able to concentrate at school. I really became very frightened when my hair fell out; I had always been so proud of my beautiful hair. My dentist told me that at the back of my teeth nearly all the enamel had disappeared, while I had very strong teeth before I developed my eating disorder. Furthermore I felt extremely tired and was always cold. It was impossible to continue this situation and I needed to ask for help, although I was also very afraid to gain weight.'

All these fears and doubts make the motivation to change highly ambivalent. The experience of a turning point, however, does not guarantee that the patient is able to take the step towards change and ask for treatment. Many eating disorder patients have several *turning points*, and each time they are really convinced that they have to change, but nevertheless find it very difficult to change because of their fears. In this stage of ambivalent motivation, much support is necessary from parents, siblings and friends for patients to overcome their fears and to ask for help.

NICOLE: 'At the worst stage of my eating disorder everybody tried to talk to me but my reaction was very negative: "leave me alone". My mother, however, never stopped talking to me. If she had not supported me I could have died. But she always said: together we will succeed. And we did succeed in the end.'

Fear of Asking for Help

Even after they realize that continuing their eating habits has severe and life-threatening consequences, it often takes a long time for patients to ask for help. They feel ashamed and are afraid of losing control over their lives.

WENDY: 'I realized that I could not continue having several binges each day. But it was very difficult for me to ask for help. I felt ashamed to admit that I took so many laxatives every day and vomited every time after a binge. My self-image was already very low, and if people knew that I had these terrible binges my self-image would become even more negative. Although there were no positive aspects left in my life I still tried to hide my problems as long as possible.'

It is very difficult to give up the eating habits, because patients feel scared of losing their self-respect, identity and control. The fear of change is often greater than the motivation to improve.

GUNN: 'In order to become motivated to change I had to believe that I had something to gain and that my life might become worthwhile. But at the most severe stage of my eating disorder I could not believe that my life might improve.'

Parents, siblings and peers can play an important role when it comes to motivating patients to change. Books about eating disorders or the Internet can also be helpful.

CINDY: 'The first book I read about anorexia nervosa was a book by Steven Levenkrohn (1979) about a girl with anorexia. My sister gave me this book, which proved very informative and opened my eyes to reality. I recognized many things. Until then I had thought that I was the only person who was dieting to such an extreme extent. This book told it like it was and frightened me. But on the other side it was also reassuring to find that I was not the only person who had this strange eating behaviour. It gave me the hope of finding a way out of this prison.'

It is especially boys and men with eating disorders who find it difficult to ask for help and sometimes have to go down a deep pit before they realize that they need help:

DAN: 'Because of frequent binging and purging I was afraid that I would not be able to finish my law degree, and would never find a job as a lawyer. Because of my binges I had huge financial debts. I was afraid I would end up as a homeless person without any income. My worst scenario was that I would steal food, be arrested, and taken to the police station so that I needed a lawyer, and then one of my fellow students would be my lawyer. That nightmare was so frightening that I overcame my shame and asked for help from one of the student counsellors. I confessed all my problems with binges and purging. Although the counsellor had never seen a male student with bulimia nervosa, he had helped many female students with this disorder. He reassured me that it was possible to overcome the binges and purging, although it would take time and energy. I was very glad that I had asked for help.'

Informative web sites about eating disorders can be very helpful, as becomes clear from the experience of Arnold, who had bulimia nervosa for many years:

> ARNOLD: 'Using the internet is anonymous and nobody would know that I was looking for information about binging and purging. So I finally had the courage to type in the word "binge". The first information I found confronted me with reality, and I became very much ashamed, because it was as if I read about my own thoughts and behaviour. However, the information also reassured me, because I read that it is not only women who can develop bulimia nervosa, but that men can get it, too. That motivated me to find help.'

Deferring treatment until eating disorder patients become motivated enough is not realistic. It is very important to motivate them not only in the period before their treatment, but also at the first stage of treatment. Strategies to motivate eating disorder patients should be the first part of the treatment (Spaans & Bloks, 2008).

Questionnaires to Improve Motivation for Treatment

To become motivated to change, eating disorder patients have to be convinced that they can improve the quality of their lives and can recover from the negative physical, psychological and social consequences of their eating disorder. They have to be convinced that they can develop self-esteem, a positive body attitude, better emotion regulation and better social relations. In order to motivate patients towards full recovery, the following questionnaires will be useful.

Questionnaire about improving eating habits

How important is it for you to improve your eating habits?

You can answer 1=no, 2=a little, 3=somewhat, 4=yes, 5=very much

1.	I want to eat healthy food	1	2	3	4	5
2.	I want to eat three meals a day	1	2	3	4	5
3.	I want to eat enough calories	1	2	3	4	5
4.	I want to reduce my binges	1	2	3	4	5
5.	I want to reduce vomiting after food intake	1	2	3	4	5
6.	I want to reduce intake of laxatives	1	2	3	4	5
7.	I want to reduce intake of diuretics	1	2	3	4	5
8.	I want to reduce intake of slimming pills	1	2	3	4	5
9.	I want to reduce physical exercises	1	2	3	4	5
10.	I want to reduce alcohol intake	1	2	3	4	5

Other factors of my eating habits I want to improve:

11.	....	1	2	3	4	5
12.	....	1	2	3	4	5
13.	....	1	2	3	4	5
14.	....	1	2	3	4	5

If your answers are 1, 2 or 3, try to find out what makes it so difficult for you to become motivated to change. If you have answered 4 or 5 to some questions you are highly motivated to change and can ask your therapist to give priority to these areas in your treatment.

Motivation for Physical Recovery

An important reason to become motivated for recovery is the wish to reduce various negative physical consequences of the eating disorder.

In order for patients to become motivated for treatment, it can be helpful to find out which physical aspects have to improve.

Questionnaire about motivation for physical recovery

How high is your motivation to improve your physical condition?

You can answer 1=no, 2=a little, 3=somewhat, 4=yes, 5=very high

1. I will feel less tired	1	2	3	4	5
2. I will have more energy	1	2	3	4	5
3. I will feel more fit	1	2	3	4	5
4. I will have no constipation anymore	1	2	3	4	5
5. I will not have problems with my bowels	1	2	3	4	5
6. I will feel less cold	1	2	3	4	5
7. I will feel no pain when I sit or lie down	1	2	3	4	5
8. I will have better skin	1	2	3	4	5
9. I will have stronger hair	1	2	3	4	5
10. I will have stronger nails	1	2	3	4	5
11. I will have healthy teeth	1	2	3	4	5

Other goals for physical improvement:

12.	....	1	2	3	4	5
13.	....	1	2	3	4	5
14.	....	1	2	3	4	5
15.	....	1	2	3	4	5

If many of your answers are 1, 2 or 3, try to find out what makes it so difficult for you to become motivated to change. If you have answered 4 or 5 to some questions, you are highly motivated to change and can ask your therapist to give priority to these areas in your treatment.

Motivation for More Self-Esteem

Eating disorders have many psychological consequences, such as developing obsessive thoughts about food and weight and fear of becoming fat or of losing control over food intake. Losing their self-esteem and self-respect scares patients. Therefore, it is important that the treatment should focus on increasing their self-esteem and self-respect.

Questionnaire about motivation for more self-esteem

How high is your motivation to improve your psychological well-being?

You can answer 1=no, 2=a little, 3=somewhat, 4=yes, 5=very high

1.	I will have more self-esteem	1	2	3	4	5
2.	My self-esteem will no longer be related to my weight	1	2	3	4	5
3.	I will have a better image of myself	1	2	3	4	5
4.	I will not punish myself after food intake	1	2	3	4	5
5.	I will have better concentration	1	2	3	4	5
6.	I will become less of a perfectionist	1	2	3	4	5
7.	I will be less afraid to fail	1	2	3	4	5
8.	I will develop a more realistic image of myself	1	2	3	4	5

Other psychological goals I would like to realize:

9.	....	1	2	3	4	5
10.	....	1	2	3	4	5
11.	....	1	2	3	4	5
12.	....	1	2	3	4	5

Discuss your answers with your therapist so that they can be taken into account in the treatment. If many of your answers are 1, 2 or 3, try to find out what makes it so difficult for you to become motivated to change. If you have answered 4 or 5 to some questions, you are highly motivated to change and can ask your therapist to give priority to these areas in your treatment.

Motivation for a more Positive Body Attitude

In order for patients to recover from their eating disorder, it is important that they no longer have a negative body attitude or feel overweight. They have to learn to accept a healthy weight and to accept their figure.

Questionnaire about motivation to improve body attitude

How high is your motivation to improve your body attitude?

You can answer 1=no, 2=a little, 3=somewhat, 4=yes, 5=very high

1.	I will no longer feel too fat	1	2	3	4	5
2.	I will have a more positive body attitude	1	2	3	4	5
3.	I will learn to accept my appearance	1	2	3	4	5
4.	I will no longer follow a diet	1	2	3	4	5
5.	I will no longer be obsessed with food and weight	1	2	3	4	5
6.	I will become more satisfied with my body	1	2	3	4	5

Other goals related to improving my body attitude:

7.	....	1	2	3	4	5
8.	....	1	2	3	4	5
9.	....	1	2	3	4	5
10.	....	1	2	3	4	5

If many of your answers are 1, 2 or 3, try to find out what makes it so difficult for you to become motivated to change. If you have answered 4 or 5 to some questions, you are highly motivated to change and can ask your therapist to give priority to these areas in your treatment.

Motivation for Better Emotion Regulation

Extreme dieting, binging and purging are often used to regulate negative emotions and to reduce feelings of stress (Fox, 2009). During the treatment, it is important to learn to recognize and to express emotions and to cope with feelings of stress.

Questionnaire about motivation for better emotion regulation

How high is your motivation to improve your emotional well-being?

You can answer 1=no, 2=a little, 3=somewhat, 4=yes, 5=very high

1.	I will have fewer negative emotions	1	2	3	4	5
2.	I will no longer be depressed	1	2	3	4	5
3.	I will have less fear of my emotions	1	2	3	4	5
4.	I will no longer avoid my emotions	1	2	3	4	5
5.	I will listen to my emotions better	1	2	3	4	5
6.	I will be able to express negative emotions	1	2	3	4	5
7.	I will be able to express positive emotions	1	2	3	4	5
8.	I will be able to cope with feelings of stress	1	2	3	4	5

Other goals related to better emotion regulation:

9.	1	2	3	4	5
10.	1	2	3	4	5
11.	1	2	3	4	5
12.	1	2	3	4	5

If many of your answers are 1, 2 or 3, try to find out what makes it so difficult for you to become motivated to change. If you have answered 4 or 5 to some questions, you are highly motivated to change and can ask your therapist to give priority to these areas in your treatment.

Motivation for Better Social Relationships

Many patients start their dieting in order to gain more self-esteem and to become more accepted by others. The effect of their eating disorder, however, is that they become more and more isolated. They fear that they may be forced to eat when they visit other people and feel very insecure about what they eat. They fear that others will discover how little they eat, or that they have binges followed by purging behaviour, such as using laxatives and vomiting or extreme exercising. Instead of becoming accepted and having more friends, they become isolated and lonely. This can motivate them to seek more social contacts.

Questionnaire about motivation for improving social relationships

How high is your motivation to improve your social relations?

You can answer 1=no, 2=a little, 3=somewhat, 4=yes, 5=very high

1. I will no longer be isolated	1	2	3	4	5
2. I will participate in social activities	1	2	3	4	5
3. I will be able to initiate contact with others	1	2	3	4	5
4. I will have some friends	1	2	3	4	5
5. I will have an intimate friend	1	2	3	4	5
6. I will improve my relationship with my parents	1	2	3	4	5
7. I will enrol in a course	1	2	3	4	5
8. I will do some voluntary work	1	2	3	4	5
9. I will apply for a job	1	2	3	4	5

Other social goals which are important for me:

10.	1	2	3	4	5

11.	....	1	2	3	4	5
12.	....	1	2	3	4	5

If your answers are 1, 2 or 3, try to find out what makes it so difficult for you to become motivated to change. If you have answered 4 or 5 to some questions, you are highly motivated to change and can ask your therapist to give priority to these areas in your treatment.

Motivation for Reducing Financial Problems

Eating disorders not only have negative physical, psychological and social consequences, but also serious financial repercussions, because of the cost of laxatives and food for binges, or because patients are unable to get a job or to hold on to one. Some patients have high debts and are forced to borrow money. Improving their financial situation can be an important trigger for motivation to recover.

Questionnaire about motivation for reducing financial problems

How high is your motivation to spend less money on your eating disorder?

You can answer 1=no, 2=a little, 3=somewhat, 4=yes, 5=very high

1.	I will spend less money on laxatives	1	2	3	4	5
2.	I will spend less money on dieting	1	2	3	4	5
3.	I will spend less money on binges	1	2	3	4	5
4.	I will spend less money on alcohol	1	2	3	4	5
5.	I will have fewer financial problems	1	2	3	4	5
6.	I will spend more money on things I like	1	2	3	4	5
7.	I will have a job to earn money	1	2	3	4	5
8.	I will have money for a holiday	1	2	3	4	5
9.	I will have money for my hobbies	1	2	3	4	5

Other financial goals which are important for me:

10.	....	1	2	3	4	5
11.	....	1	2	3	4	5
12.	....	1	2	3	4	5

If your answers are 1, 2 or 3, try to find out what makes it so difficult for you to become motivated to change. If you have answered 4 or 5 to some questions, you are highly motivated to change and can ask your therapist to give priority to these areas in your treatment.

Summary

This chapter discussed the reasons why it is so difficult for eating disorder patients to become motivated to change. Only when they are confronted with severe negative physical, psychological, emotional, social and financial consequences does their motivation to change increase. For most patients, the motivation to change their eating habits is very ambivalent. They fear that when they have to eat more and gain weight they will lose their self-respect and the control over their lives.

In order to motivate them to change, it is important that they learn that by giving up their eating habits they can gain a better life and future. They have to realize that treatment can bring them not only better physical health, but also more self-esteem, a more positive body attitude, better emotion regulation, more effective coping strategies and better social contacts. In the following chapters, recovered patients recount how they succeeded in overcoming their disorder.

In Figure 4.1, the stages in the development of, and recovery from, an eating disorder are presented.

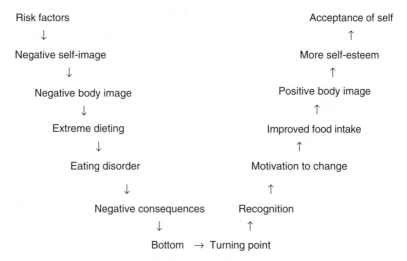

Figure 4.1   Stages in the development of, and recovery from, an eating disorder.

5

Normalizing Eating Habits

Introduction

For a long time, the idea among professionals was that eating disorder patients recovered when their food intake and weight had been normalized. However, many studies have shown that the risk of relapse is very high when the visible symptoms of the eating disorder have reduced but the underlying psychological factors have not improved (Fennig, Fennig, & Roe, 2002; Strober, Freeman, & Morrell, 1997). Moreover, eating disorder patients often feel bad after a treatment which is exclusively focused at increasing food intake and weight because they lose their self-respect and control over their body. They find it difficult to accept their *bloated* body and run the risk of becoming depressed and even developing suicidal thoughts. When patients have a very negative view of their treatment, they lose all trust in the therapy (Noordenbos, Oldenhave, Muschter, & Terpstra, 2002).

Research into the effectiveness of the treatment of eating disorders has clearly shown that in eating disorder patients, the body and mind cannot be separated but are closely related and function as an integrative system. Treatment directed only at recovery from the physical consequences of the eating disorder is ineffective, because patients continue to have disturbed cognitions about food and weight and remain obsessed by food and weight. However, therapy that is directed only at changing their cognitions without improving food intake and weight is not effective either. When the body is in a very bad condition because of severe starvation, eating disorder patients can no longer think clearly and thus psychotherapy is ineffective.

Recovery from Eating Disorders: A Guide for Clinicians and Their Clients,
First Edition. Greta Noordenbos.
© 2013 John Wiley & Sons, Ltd. Published 2013 by John Wiley & Sons, Ltd.

In this chapter, recovered eating disorder patients relate how they managed to normalize their eating habits and to change all kinds of disturbed cognitions about food and weight.

Overcoming the Fear of Increasing Food Intake

For patients with anorexia nervosa, one of the most difficult problems is to reduce the *fear* of increasing their food intake and weight. After months or even years of anorectic eating habits, they lose all conception of what constitutes a healthy amount of food.

For bulimic patients, it is important to reduce the number of binges and to learn to eat normal amounts of food without vomiting, using laxatives or exercising. Moreover, eating disorder patients who get addicted to alcohol to lessen their negative emotions should reduce alcohol consumption.

> WENDY: 'When I started my treatment I was so afraid of becoming fat. For me it seemed impossible to increase my weight in a short time. My fear of food was so great that I panicked when I had to eat what the clinic put on my plate. It felt as if I was drowning in a sea of fear.'

During the first period of increasing food intake and weight, eating disorder patients have emotional problems and feel scared and guilty. They view themselves in a very negative light and feel bad about their body being controlled by others. Losing control over food is felt as losing control over themselves. This can cause panic:

> BEA: 'When I lost the control over my food and weight I had the feeling that my sense of *self* had completely disappeared. It was as if I had jumped into the water while having no arms or legs, so that I could not swim. I panicked because I felt I was drowning. Before you jump into the water you first have to learn to swim. I first needed to have a basic feeling of control over my life, before I was able to change my food intake and weight. Without a basic feeling of control I was not able to change my slimming behaviour, because I was so afraid that my sense of self might disappear completely. It was a choice between existing as a subject with control over my life, or becoming an object which was controlled by others. I was scared of losing all sense of self and becoming just an object.'

These quotes make it clear that the fear of losing control over food intake is not only related to the fear of gaining weight but is also an existential fear of losing all sense of being an autonomous subject and becoming an object for others.

RACHEL: 'When the nurse forced me to eat all the food on my plate I was afraid to lose the last part of my identity. If I could not control my food I would completely lose myself and become "nobody".'

Increasing food intake is closely related to patients' fear of losing control over their lives and hence their identity and sense of self. Due to this, forced feeding has to be prevented at all cost.

Psycho-education about the need for more food and the physical consequences of increasing food intake and weight is very helpful.

JODY: 'In the first period of increasing food intake my stomach felt extremely full and I suffered a lot from constipation. At that stage I felt very fat, which was extremely frightening for me. In the therapy I learned that constipation was quite normal for patients who had used laxatives for a long time. Because of all these laxatives my bowels did not work any more and had to be activated. The therapist informed me that after some weeks my intestines would function properly again. Although the first day of each new food programme was very difficult and made me panic, I slowly learned to be less afraid. When my bowels started working again and my weight increased slowly I learned to accept my weight.'

In the first period of treatment, patients have to adjust to eating more food at regular intervals. For eating disorder patients, it is very important to retain a feeling of control over their food intake. A treatment programme in which the amount of food is increased step by step is very helpful to get accustomed to the greater amounts of food and increased weight.

RUTH: 'What was very important for me was that the schedule for food intake was very regular and that I was able to get slowly accustomed to eating more. Each week I received a new food schedule and during that week I was able to get used to the larger amounts of food. Food intake increased step by step. For me that was a safe and effective strategy. My weight increased only slowly, and this gave me time to get accustomed to my greater weight.'

THALIA: 'For me it was very important that I could keep some control over my food intake and could learn to eat more step by step. I was happy that I was never forced to eat.'

CAROL: 'I had to learn all over again how much food was necessary to nourish my body. In the treatment I was given a programme listing when and what to eat. That programme was very important for me. If they had asked me to choose my own food I would never have succeeded in eating healthy amounts of food, because my ideas about food were completely disturbed.'

JOYCE: 'It took me several years to increase my food consumption, starting with food which was "safe" for me. When I developed more self-esteem I became less afraid of "new" food and had the courage to try new food which had been "forbidden" for many years. Finally I even dared to eat oily fish and I was able to integrate that into my weekly menu.'

Increasing food intake takes much time and requires patience from therapists and family. But in the long run, the strategy of slowly increasing food intake and weight is much more effective than a strategy in which weight gain has to be realized in a short period.

Changing Cognitions about Food

Anorectic patients often know the number of calories of all kinds of food and are always counting calories.

SUZAN: 'Calorie tables were a disaster for me. When I knew the number of calories in vegetables and fruit I hardly dared to eat anything.'

Eating disorder patients are completely *brainwashed* by the idea that *calories are fat and fat is bad*. Having repeated this dogma for many years, they are unable to change this belief in a short period. Anorectic patients often find it difficult to believe that the *dogma* that calories make them fat is a misconception.

The definition of a calorie does not refer to something that produces fat, but to something that produces energy. Calories are an important source of energy for the body and the brain. They are necessary for the growth of nails and hair and to replace skin cells. Calories produce the energy needed for walking, bicycling, reading, talking over the phone, texting and so on. Without the intake of calories, the body cannot develop energy for physical, psychological and social activities and becomes exhausted. Consuming enough calories is necessary not only for healthy physical functioning but also for psychological well-being. The intake of sufficient calories is a necessary condition to be in a positive frame of mind.

Only when the intake of calories is higher than the amount of calories burned will the surplus be stored in fat cells. Anorectic patients, however, burn many more calories than they consume, and thus their body becomes exhausted and severely emaciated. They have to be told that physical organs need energy from calories to function in a healthy way.

Bulimic patients too end up exhausting their body completely by vomiting after every binge, or by using laxatives and exercising in an extreme way.

Eating disorder patients often have very disturbed ideas about weight increase and think that calories are directly transformed into fat cells or that their body can function without any fat intake. Each body needs the intake of healthy fat to develop energy for all the basic organs, a regular heartbeat and a normal body temperature. The brain, too, needs fat intake in order to function optimally. Some vitamins, such as A, D, E and K as well as beta carotene, can only be absorbed by fat (Tenwolde, 2000). Fat cells are also necessary for the production of hormones. According to Tenwolde, around 6% of the daily food intake should contain healthy fat. It is important for eating disorder patients to change their distorted cognitions about fat intake and to learn to accept having to eat healthy fat.

Many eating disorder patients are vegetarians because they think they lose more weight when they do not eat meat. However, there is a lack of amino acids in their diet unless they eat enough grain products such as corn, peas and beans (Tenwolde, 2000).

Eating disorder patients have severely disturbed ideas about food and should be guided about the healthy nutrients necessary to nourish their body. To change their distorted ideas about food, psycho-education and cognitive behaviour therapy are important.

ANN: 'The information I got from my dietician was quite revealing, because I realized that my body was severely undernourished. She compared my body to a car with an empty tank, so that the motor stagnated if you tried to drive it. In order to repair the car a total overhaul was necessary. She compared the nourishing programme for me to charging the car battery. Only after charging my physical battery would I be able to drive again. This information was very useful for me and helped me to restore my body.'

MARY: 'I had to change all my opinions about food. I always thought that each calorie would be transformed into fat cells. I thought that every calorie would make me fat, and I wanted to prevent that at any price. I never realized that my brain needed calories in order to be able to think and learn. Having exhausted my body for many years I was no longer able to concentrate on my lessons and for the first time in my life I had low grades. I felt ashamed of my failure at school, which did not help my self-esteem. But my body did not function any more either. My nails became brittle, and I had always liked my long nails. My physical condition was very bad. I felt weak and often fainted. When I started to eat more I got more energy and was able to concentrate much better. I was able to study again and I was very happy when I got good grades for my exam.'

GEORG: 'In my treatment I learned to eat healthy amounts of different kinds of food, without always counting how many calories I ate. I learned that when I eat enough and healthy food I can keep a stable weight within a normal range.'

CAROL: 'I learned that food and beauty are closely connected. Food can make you beautiful because of the vitamins, minerals and healthy fat. My skin, hair and nails are now in a much better condition. I even take omega-3 capsules and look much better.'

Three Regular Meals a Day

Many eating disorder patients skip their breakfast because they think it helps them to lose weight. This, however, is a serious misconception. In the morning, the body needs food in order to develop enough energy. Skipping breakfast makes people feel hungry and irritated during the morning, and they start to think about food, which lessens the ability to concentrate.

MARISKA: 'For many years I trained myself to take only two meals a day: a light lunch in the afternoon and a small dinner in the evening. I only took small portions of food. I thought I would lose weight when I skipped my breakfast. In the clinic, however, I learned that this increased the risk of having a binge. I was always extremely hungry in the morning, and often lost control during lunch time and ate much more than I wanted to eat. During the treatment I had to start each day with a healthy and nourishing breakfast. At first I found it very scary to eat so many calories early in the morning. But after some weeks I noted that my urge to eat during lunch time had reduced substantially. In the treatment it was no longer allowed to vomit in the evening so my body had time to digest the food, and I was less hungry in the morning. I felt that I could concentrate much better and felt more relaxed and less stressed and irritated. When I came home after my job I no longer felt the urge to binge and to vomit. I feel so much better now.'

NATASCHA: 'For me it was normal to go to my job without breakfast. In the therapy, however, I had to take breakfast, lunch and dinner at regular times and some healthy snacks in-between. After several months I felt much more relaxed and had more energy. Sometimes I do not have enough time for my breakfast, but then I get extremely hungry at the end of the morning and lose my concentration and become irritated. This shows me how important it is to have breakfast before I leave for work. I will never return to that dark period in my life when I became extremely hungry in the morning and always thought about food, and finally ended up having a binge followed by purging. That was an extremely bad period.'

FARIDA: 'In the treatment I learned to listen to my body and to notice when I was hungry and needed to eat, instead of ignoring the signals of my body. Now I eat regularly and I always have breakfast, lunch and dinner, and some healthy snacks in-between. I learned that I can trust my body and my feelings of hunger and satiety. These feelings are no longer threatening for me.'

Regular Mealtimes

Eating disorder patients not only lose track about what constitutes healthy amounts of food, but also have a very disturbed mealtime schedule. They develop compulsive rules about what, when and where to eat. If they are unable to keep to their strict schedule, they panic and lose control over their food intake.

> JEANNE: 'I only allowed myself breakfast between 8.00 and 8.10 in the morning. Then I had to cycle to school. Within those ten minutes I ate two dry crackers and a cup of tea, dunking the crackers in the tea. But sometimes I slept a little longer, which meant going without breakfast because I had to leave for school at 8.10 exactly and I did not want to miss my first lesson. But that was not the real reason, because in the evening I also had a very strict schedule for a very short dinner, and I did not need to go to school. In the evening I wanted to leave the dinner table no later than 7 p.m. If we had not finished dinner at that time I became very nervous and irritated. My compulsive behaviour drove my mother crazy. For many years we did not have dinner in a relaxed way and were always quarreling at the table.'

Psycho-education and cognitive behaviour therapy can help to change distorted thoughts about food. After they have followed a healthy schedule of food intake, patients' fear slowly reduces, and they become more relaxed about what, when and where to eat.

> ESTHER: 'In the treatment I learned to relax much more and to let go of my obsessive-compulsive eating schedule. I learned that no disasters would happen if I had my breakfast, lunch or dinner a bit earlier or later. I learned that my feelings of fear and panic were feelings within myself which had nothing to do with the strict mealtimes. At the clinic I had to tone down my obsessive thoughts about eating times.'

To compensate for their binges, bulimic patients often eat very little during daytime. This fasting behaviour, however, increases the risk of a new binge in the evening. To change this pattern, it is necessary for patients to develop a regular eating pattern of three nourishing meals a day: breakfast, lunch and dinner, and some snacks in-between. Taking regular meals reduces the physical urge towards binging because the stomach is less empty and the body is better nourished.

> FERNANDO: 'When I started to follow more regular meal times my urge to have a binge decreased substantially. I was less hungry, irritated and stressed. That made me feel much better about myself. Having regular meals and enough food was an important strategy to reduce my binges.'

Reduction of Binges

For patients with bulimia nervosa, the first aim of the treatment is to reduce binging and purging. This behaviour has extreme negative physical effects, such as constipation, sore throat, gland problems, pain in the stomach or even a stomach rupture (Tenwolde, 2000). Although bulimic patients often try to stop having binges, they seldom succeed. Ellen often thought that she had had her last binge, but then could not resist the urge to have another.

> ELLEN: 'I often thought: this is my last binge, tomorrow I will stop completely. For my "last" binge I collected all kinds of food from the kitchens in the student house where I lived. I really thought that this was my last binge and allowed myself to eat everything: sugar, butter, cream, chocolate, etcetera. At the end I felt completely bloated and exhausted. I could not vomit any more, so I took all the laxatives I had left, I guess more than 20 pills. I really thought that this was my last binge so that I never needed to take laxatives again. But only a week later I felt an extreme urge to have a binge and could no longer control my food intake. Many times I thought: this is the last time, and only a week later had another binge. In the end it took me many years to get rid of my binges.'

Ellen makes clear that it is not realistic to think that it is possible to quit binging within a short time, even when motivation is very high.

> ELLEN: 'When I was admitted to the Clinic for Eating Disorders I learned to have regular mealtimes and it seemed as if my binges were over. In that clinic I made great progress and everything seemed to go very well, but nobody knew that I had binges in the weekends, because I hid them from others as much as possible. I really had a double life in that period. When I was home the stress had become so extreme that I really needed to have a binge. When I came back to the clinic on Monday nobody knew what had happened at home, and I followed the day programme exactly, so that they thought I had made a lot of progress. But each weekend when I came home I had a binge. That went on for months.'

Keeping a diary about when, where, why and what patients eat is a helpful strategy to get insight into the relation between food and emotions.

TATIANA: 'During my treatment I had to keep a diary about my food intake. On the left side I had to note when I ate and what, and on the right side I had to describe my feelings and emotions. This was very revealing, because it gave me a clear insight into how much I ate. I saw a clear connection between my food intake and my feelings. Before a binge I often felt very pessimistic and restless. After binging and purging I felt relieved, but also very guilty. In the treatment I had to analyse what had triggered my binge, and what was the source of my negative feelings and stress. I realized that in my job I often felt irritated and angry, but did not dare to say anything. All the stress was stored up in my body. In the therapy I learned that it was much better to release my stress at an earlier stage. I also had to practice alternative strategies when I felt highly stressed. When the stress became very high and I felt the urge to have a binge, I had to leave my house and run for a while before I was allowed to have a binge. Running helped to reduce my stress. After some months the need to have a binge had substantially diminished.'

Negative emotions and stress play an important role in having binges. To reduce binges, it is important to find out which situations and emotions precede a binge and to explore how negative thoughts and emotions can be reduced in a healthy way.

MARIA: 'My binges are connected with the feeling that I have a deep emotional hole in myself, which might have been created by my parents who often were not able to comfort me when I needed them. I tried to fill this emotional hole in myself with plenty of food, but that worked only for a short time. Only when I received attention from a therapist, who was able to listen to all my sad experiences, did I discover that my emotional hole could be filled by talking about my emotions to somebody who mirrored my feelings and reacted with compassion to all my negative emotions. Learning to express my emotions and receiving adequate feedback from my therapist helped me to accept my negative emotions instead of reducing them by having binges. That therapist was very important for me.'

In order to reduce their binges, it is important that patients develop alternative coping strategies to regulate negative emotions and stress.

JOSINE: 'In the clinic for eating disorders I learned to reduce my binges. They used a very strict programme consisting of three regular meals and some snacks. In the first phase I was not allowed go home in the weekends. This period in the clinic was terrible because my body craved for a binge. I even had all kinds of physical reactions, such as trembling, sweating and heart palpitations. The sweating and trembling were so bad that I became very restless and urgently needed a binge. I really had to fight very hard against that urge. But this therapy was my last chance and I really wanted to stop having binges. In that clinic I learned to talk about all my emotions. When I felt the urge to have a binge I had to run for 10 to 15 minutes. In that way I succeeded in cutting down my binges.'

For many bulimic patients, it is very difficult stop binging, and it might be more realistic for them to sometimes have a binge when the stress becomes too high. After each binge, it is important to analyse which conditions triggered the binge, and whether in the future alternative strategies can be used in order to reduce stress.

ELISA: 'In the last weeks of my time at the clinic I was allowed to go home during the weekends, and unfortunately I often had a binge at home. But this binge was less extreme than before I went into the clinic. After each binge I felt very negative and frustrated, but it also brought some relief from stress. So, in the end I no longer struggled against having a binge, and accepted that I would sometimes have one. That idea already reduced my stress and the number of binges.'

It is not only the idea that it is unrealistic to put a stop to all binging in a short period that reduces patients' stress, but also the fact that they no longer have to hide their secret binges.

DANNY: 'I learned that when I had a binge it was helpful to mention it to a person I could trust. This reduced the stress of hiding my binge from others and having a "double life". I also learned that I did not need to feel so bad about binging. I learned to accept that it happened now and then. This relaxed me much more than constantly struggling against my binges, because that produced extra stress. Now I accept that I can have a binge when the stress becomes very high. After a binge I always analyse which feelings I had before, during and after, in my diary. I also learned to talk about my binge with one of my best friends, so that I no longer have to hide my feelings and emotions.'

Reduction of Purging

An important strategy to reduce the physical urge to have a binge is to *reduce purging behaviour* after the binge, such as vomiting, using laxatives or exercising. Purging behaviour is physically exhausting because the body does not have enough time to absorb the food, leading to undernourishment. The body urgently needs food, which provokes a new binge. To break this vicious circle, purging behaviour has to be reduced.

GWEN: 'In the clinic for eating disorders it was not allowed to vomit after a meal. Going to the toilet was forbidden for one hour after a meal. That was terrible, because without vomiting I was scared of becoming fat. But in the second week my urge to have a binge became less and I felt more relaxed. I learned that if I had three regular meals a day and did not vomit or use laxatives, my body was nourished much better and the physical need for a binge would become less. After a few months I had stopped having binges, and I no longer felt that extreme need.'

VICKY: 'Sometimes when I ate more than I intended I longed to vomit, but I knew that this was a very bad strategy, because after vomiting you run the risk of having another binge. I really wanted to get out of that vicious circle of binging and vomiting. I managed to eat three regular meals and some snacks in-between, which was very helpful. Only when I have a very stressful day I sometimes have a binge, but in that case I force myself not to vomit in order to prevent a new binge. I also learned to use better strategies to reduce stress, such as talking about my feelings, writing in my diary, jogging etcetera.'

Bulimic patients often are afraid that their weight might increase when they stop to vomit.

PETER: 'Because of my binges my weight had increased. I was afraid that if I stopped purging I might gain even more weight. I was surprised to find that my weight did not increase when I ate three regular meals and stopped vomiting. That was very stimulating.'

If the bulimia has lasted many months or even years, it is very difficult to stop the vomiting in a few days or weeks. A gradual reduction is more realistic than to stop all vomiting at once. Slowly cutting back the purging behaviour gives less stress than to stop all purging at once.

ADINA: 'When I completely forbade myself to binge and purge I became extremely stressed and had to struggle against the binges and purging behaviour. This was a struggle I always lost, so that I felt a complete failure. But when I accepted that I could have a binge and vomit once a week my stress became much lower. There were even some weeks in which I did not have a binge.'

ESTHER: 'By accepting my binges and vomiting I no longer had to struggle all day to prevent myself from having a binge. That helped me to reduce my binges to eating smaller portions, and I also managed to reduce the urge to vomit. I was very glad that I did not have to vomit any more, because I hated it: it was painful, disgusting and gave me very bad feelings about myself. Moreover, my teeth had become seriously damaged. When I found I was able to reduce my binging and purging behaviour I became proud of myself. I really was on the way to recovery and could now spend my energy and money on more interesting things.'

Healthy and Sufficient Food

Eating disorder patients develop very disturbed ideas about food. Anorectic patients allow themselves to eat only very small portions containing very few calories.

WENDELA: 'My ideas about what was enough food were completely disturbed in the period of my anorexia. When the dietician told me what I needed to eat for breakfast, I thought the number of calories in this breakfast would be enough for the whole day. But she insisted that this was a healthy breakfast for young women. For me it was a real struggle to eat that much each morning. Now I have recovered from my eating disorder, and I cannot understand why I ate so little during all the years in which I had anorexia.'

If patients are to learn to eat healthy amounts of food, the advice of a dietician is very important to develop a strategy to increase food intake gradually. A dietician can give objective information about the amount of food necessary to feed the body and can draw up a programme of balanced meals containing essential nutrients.

ALICE: 'For years I had indoctrinated myself with the dogma that eating fewer calories is good and more calories is bad. When I ate more calories I immediately felt guilty, because it meant I had sinned against one of the basic dogmas of my strict diet. Finally I was completely at a loss as to what was enough food for me. I only knew that it was "good" to have a very strict diet with very few calories. At the clinic, however, I learned that my body needs much more calories than I allowed myself to eat. Although I *knew* this in a rational way, my *feelings* about food were very negative and I always felt very guilty after each meal. Even when I ate an apple as a snack I felt guilty and criticized myself for eating too much. In the treatment I was asked to analyse whether it was fair to have these feelings of guilt after eating an apple. I learned that this was not fair and it was not right to punish myself by extreme exercising. Every time I felt guilty or bad after a meal I was asked to analyse whether these feelings were right and fair. I learned to defend myself against my negative thoughts and feelings. For example: "I feel guilty, but why? Did I really eat too much when I just ate a normal meal?" I became angry about my feelings of guilt and said to myself: "Stop that, it is not fair!" This helped me to change my cognitions about food, and now I feel much less negative after dinner.'

Reduction of Laxatives, Diuretics and Slimming Pills

Patients with anorexia and bulimia often use laxatives in order to get the food out of their body as soon as possible and to prevent weight gain. They start with only a few laxatives, but gradually take more and more. This results in their bowels becoming inactive and eventually to constipation, which stimulates them to take even more laxatives. Finally, they get into a vicious circle of taking laxatives, becoming constipated, taking more laxatives and so on.

Using a large amount of laxatives is quite dangerous and can have many side effects such as diarrhoea, inactive bowels, constipation, haemorrhoids, bulging of the rectum because of severe pressure, extreme stomach pains, distortion of the intestinal tube and intestinal bleeding. The metabolism of the body is reduced and the body becomes undernourished (Tenwolde, 2000). To recover from the physical consequences of laxative abuse, it is important to reduce the intake of laxatives. The following strategies may be used.

A: *Stopping the laxatives immediately*

This strategy is difficult for patients because their bowels have become inactive and they suffer from constipation. To reduce constipation, it is helpful to eat vegetables, fruits, fibres and bran and to drink enough water. After a few days, the bowels become activated so that other food can be introduced into the menu. This strategy is possible in a clinic for eating disorders, where therapists can give much attention to the patients.

TAMARA: 'At first I had many problems, and my stomach felt very bloated after dinner. Although I ate only vegetables and fruit and drank a lot of water I had severe constipation. I thought that everybody could see that I my stomach was huge. That was terrible. My constipation disappeared gradually and my intestines became reactivated. That gave me the feeling that my body could recover. It really was a miracle for me that after all those years of considerable laxative abuse my intestines were able to function again. Before the treatment I was afraid that I would have to use laxatives for the rest of my life. That was also a financial problem because laxatives were not cheap. Now I feel so much better and I can spend all my money on other things.'

For most patients, however, the strategy to stop taking laxatives completely all of a sudden is extremely difficult. It is more realistic for them to reduce the intake of laxatives gradually.

B: *Gradual reduction of laxatives*

In this strategy, the number of laxatives is reduced in a gradual way, so that patients can get accustomed to taking fewer and fewer laxatives and finally stop taking them altogether. This method can take several weeks.

> YVONNE: 'Sometimes I was constipated, and then immediately turned to laxatives. But because of the pain and costs I really tried to reduce the amount of laxatives I took. Now when I am constipated I try to eat more fruits and vegetables and drink more water so that constipation disappears within a few days. I gradually reduced my laxative intake, and finally I threw away the last box of pills myself. That was an important decision and a huge step forward in my life. My body is now healthy and functioning normally. With the money I saved I was able to buy myself a nice present. I am very proud of this result.'

The same strategy of cutting back gradually can be used to reduce the intake of diuretics, which are often used by anorectic patients in order to lose weight. Diuretics have many negative consequences, such as dehydration of the body, which is harmful for the kidneys.

Most slimming pills are some kind of laxatives or diuretics and have comparable consequences. When patients have got accustomed to taking slimming pills, a gradual reduction is preferable. The same problems with constipation are found after reducing the intake of slimming pills, and the same solutions are relevant, such as consuming fruits and vegetables and drinking enough water.

Drinking Water and other Liquids

In the treatment of eating disorders, most attention is given to food. It is, however, equally important to improve the intake of water and other liquids. An adult needs around 2.8 litres of liquid a day. This leaves the body via breathing, transpiration, and urinating and defecation (Tenwolde, 2000).

The kidneys transport around 2.5 litres of liquid every day. However, when more than 4 litres of water is consumed in a day, the kidneys become overloaded.

In many anorectic and bulimic patients, the intake of water is disturbed. Some anorectic patients drink very little liquid, because they are afraid of an increased calorie intake. If anorectic patients do not drink enough, they run the risk of dehydration, especially when they take laxatives or vomit. Patients with bulimia nervosa often drink much water in order to vomit regularly, but drinking too much water can also be dangerous and toxic (Tenwolde, 2000).

It is important to ask how much water and other liquids the patients drink. Do they drink more or less than is healthy? Do they drink a lot of water to reduce their feelings of hunger or because they want to vomit? Psycho-education and cognitive behaviour therapy are very useful in reducing disturbed cognitions about the consumption of water and other liquids.

No Extreme Exercising

Some eating disorder patients who successfully manage to reduce their vomiting, laxatives and diuretics intake nevertheless seek compensation in excessive exercising and can become completely obsessed by this in order to burn calories.

HELENA: 'The treatment in the hospital was terrible so I tried to get out of there as soon as possible and I ate everything they offered me. I was very afraid to gain weight, so I tried to exercise whenever possible. I ran up and down the hospital stairs. After a while my therapist saw me and forbade me to continue my exercising regime. I then tried to hide my workouts by staying inside the toilet where I did all kind of exercises. Even in bed I was exercising. Instead of counting calories, I counted my exercises: I had to do various kinds at least a hundred times a day. So my obsession with calories was followed by obsessive exercising.'

MARCEL: 'In the hospital they did not understand why my weight did not increase, because they saw me eat everything they put on my plate. For that reason they allowed me to leave the hospital, although my weight was still very low. At home I had much more opportunity to exercise and after some weeks I again had lost much weight, so my mother became alarmed and contacted our GP, who referred me to the hospital again.'

WENDELA: 'I realized that I did not make any progress and had just exchanged obsessively counting calories for obsessively counting exercises. My body was exhausted and one evening I fainted. Then I realized that I could not continue with this "solution". Fortunately I found what for me was a very good therapy, called "body-focused therapy". There I learned to listen to my body much better. Slowly I learned to accept my body and no longer to focus on all the negative aspects. I have been in therapy for one year now and feel so much better. Now I only do physical activities together with others. Each weekend I take a long walk together with a friend, which prevents me from becoming isolated and obsessed by exercising. When I walk too fast my friend corrects me and says that exercising is just for pleasure and not for burning calories.'

GWEN: 'My urge for extreme exercising only gradually disappeared when I was able to reduce my binging and became less afraid to gain weight. I still do some exercises each day, but that is just to keep my body in good condition, not because I want to lose weight and to burn calories.'

Treatment of Comorbidity

Many eating disorder patients have comorbid complaints, such as an obsessive-compulsive disorder, a fear disorder, depression, auto-mutilation or a post-traumatic stress disorder (Agras & Apple, 1997). These comorbid disorders can date from before the eating disorder or can exist alongside it, but it is also possible that the comorbidity only becomes visible after the eating disorder symptoms have disappeared. The eating disorder might have functioned as a way to suppress the comorbid disorder. It is important that the comorbid disorder is treated by a therapist who is specialized in that particular complaint.

Questionnaire about improving eating habits

In the following questionnaire, you can indicate whether your eating habits have improved.

You can answer 1=not at all, 2=very little, 3=somewhat, 4=much, 5=very much

1.	I have my meals regularly	1	2	3	4	5
2.	I eat three meals a day	1	2	3	4	5
3.	I consume enough calories	1	2	3	4	5
4.	I have reduced my binges	1	2	3	4	5
5.	I have reduced vomiting after food intake	1	2	3	4	5
6.	I have reduced the intake of laxatives	1	2	3	4	5
7.	I have reduced the intake of diuretics	1	2	3	4	5

8.	I have reduced the intake of slimming pills	1	2	3	4	5
9.	I have reduced my physical exercises	1	2	3	4	5
10.	I have reduced my alcohol intake	1	2	3	4	5

Other aspects of my eating habits which have improved:

11.	....	1	2	3	4	5
12.	....	1	2	3	4	5
13.	....	1	2	3	4	5
14.	....	1	2	3	4	5

If you answered some questions with 1, 2 or 3, you can discuss your answers with your therapist, so that these areas can be taken into account and receive extra attention in the treatment. If you answered some questions with a 4 or 5, you have improved and try to continue in the same manner.

Summary

To recover from an eating disorder, it is important that patients are no longer afraid to eat in a healthy and regular way. Anorectic patients have to increase their food intake and weight. They have to learn what is healthy food and what their body needs. For patients with bulimia nervosa, the first goal is to reduce their binging and purging behaviour, such as vomiting, using laxatives, diuretics and slimming pills, or extreme exercising.

As long as patients are afraid of eating in a more healthy way, gaining weight and becoming fat, they run the risk of a relapse. For full recovery, their food intake has to become healthy and regular. This is important in order to reduce the physical consequences of their disturbed eating habits. However, to be able to eat in a healthy way, the factors underlying their eating disorder also have to be addressed in the treatment, such as negative body and self- evaluation, dysfunctional emotion regulation and lack of social coping strategies. These goals for recovery are described in the following chapters.

6

A Positive Body Attitude

Introduction

One of the main risk factors for developing an eating disorder is a negative body attitude and feeling fat. If this attitude does not change, the risk of relapse is very high. For full recovery, a positive evaluation of one's body is very important. A major goal in treatment is for patients to learn to accept their body and no longer see it as too fat. They have to learn to focus on the positive aspects of their body instead of only seeing the negative aspects. They have to learn that dieting is not the solution to their negative self- and body evaluation. In this chapter, recovered patients describe how they learned to develop a positive attitude towards their body.

Not Feeling Fat

Most eating disorder patients start a diet because they feel too fat or are afraid to become fat. Even when there is no objective reason for dieting, it is their subjective feeling that they are fat or might become fat which motivates them to diet. Feeling fat is closely connected with all kinds of negative stereotypes, such as not being attractive and sexy, being less intelligent, lazy, ugly and so on. The lower patients' self- and body evaluation, the higher their fear of becoming fat and being criticized or teased. Their fear of being rejected by others is very high (Bruch, 1978; Pinhas, Toner, Garfinkel, & Stuckless, 1999).

Recovery from Eating Disorders: A Guide for Clinicians and Their Clients, First Edition. Greta Noordenbos.
© 2013 John Wiley & Sons, Ltd. Published 2013 by John Wiley & Sons, Ltd.

Although many people try to avoid becoming overweight or obese, and follow a diet in order to lose weight, most of them stop when they have reached their target weight. This, however, is not the case with anorectic patients, who continue their slimming behaviour even after severe weight loss. How they see their weight and food intake is illustrated clearly in the following Quote:

ANGELA: 'My self-respect was closely linked to dieting and slimming. Gaining weight was extremely threatening, because it meant I had failed and might be rejected by others. They would surely see me as stupid, lazy and ugly. I had to prevent that at any cost. All I could think was that if I ate more, my weight would increase and that would be a very bad thing. I absolutely could not see that I had already lost much weight. Even when I was severely emaciated I was still afraid to become fat if I only ate one extra piece of bread.'

The fear of gaining weight is often so strong that it takes a long time to reduce that feeling:

RUBY: 'My fear of gaining weight and becoming fat disappeared only very late, when I had a healthy and stable weight and discovered that my weight did not increase when I ate in a healthy way. Physically I felt much better, but deep inside me I was always afraid to gain weight, because gaining weight was strongly related to negative feelings and the fear of negative reactions from others.'

It takes much time before anorectic patients realize that they have become extremely thin. For Mariska, a full-length mirror helped her to see how emaciated her body was:

MARISKA: 'I always focused my perception on certain parts of my body which I saw as too fat. I could never see what others saw. When I looked in a mirror in which I could see my whole body from head to feet, I was able to see myself in the right proportions. For the first time I could see that my body was much thinner than I thought it was. However, I still felt fat. That was very strange.'

FRANCIS: 'It took a long time before that feeling of being fat disappeared. I was able to lose my fear of gaining weight only when I had developed more self-esteem and when my self-respect was no longer based on my weight. Now, if my weight increases a little I no longer feel I have failed. I learned that nobody sees the difference when your weight increases by a few ounces. Moreover, I want to be valued for the person I am, and not for my weight!'

No Longer Obsessed by Food and Weight

When eating disorder patients have learned to eat enough and have reached a healthy weight, this does not yet imply that they are fully recovered, because they can still have obsessive thoughts about food and weight.

RACHEL: 'After the hospital treatment I decided that I never again wanted to be admitted to a clinic, and I did everything to eat enough and to keep my weight at a normal level. My parents thought that I had recovered from my eating disorder because I ate normal amounts of food and my weight was normal. But in my mind I constantly thought about food and weight. I had very strict rules for myself and never could eat in a relaxed way. I always ate the same amount of food and whenever my parents changed something in my meals I really panicked, because I was afraid that this food might make me fat. That was still my biggest fear: to became fat and to be teased by my schoolmates.'

JENNIFER: 'Although my weight had increased to within a normal range I was always thinking about food and weight. I had many strict rules about my food intake. I was unable to eat in a relaxed way and was always afraid that my weight might increase. However, I took care that my weight did not become too low, because I never again wanted to be admitted to a hospital. Although my food intake and weight seemed healthy, my thoughts were still those of an anorectic patient and I was obsessed by food and weight.'

CAROLA: 'I was discharged from the hospital because my weight was no longer too low and I ate three meals a day. My mother kept me under strict surveillance to prevent me from vomiting or taking laxatives after a meal. But I still was afraid I might become fat. Then I discovered that I could control my weight by exercising. Each day I had to run at least five miles, and when the weather was bad I had to do 100 pushups in my room. I was obsessed with these exercises and had many strict rules and rituals, which took much time. My body and weight seemed to have recovered, but in my mind I was obsessed by controlling my weight. I really was a prisoner of my thoughts about food and weight.'

These quotes from Rachel, Jennifer and Carola clearly show that a normal body weight does not guarantee a positive body evaluation. Many anorectic patients whose weight increases to a normal level find it difficult to get accustomed to their increased body weight.

For full recovery, it is not only necessary that food intake and weight be normalized but also that patients become less obsessed by food and weight and are able to eat without counting calories or fearing weight increase.

VICKY: 'I am so glad that I can enjoy meals and have dinner in a restaurant with friends. I no longer want to be ruled by the scales. I feel satisfied with my figure and no longer try to realize an unrealistic body ideal. Food and weight no longer dominate my life.'

Linda managed to become more relaxed about food and weight. She said that she had been obsessed by food and weight for many years, until she went to a tropical country in Asia where she visited her family. There she was able to change her compulsive exercising and became much more relaxed about food and weight.

LINDA: 'It was extremely warm in the country where my family lived so that I was not able to do my runs. The heat made me slow and relaxed. My aunt and uncle did not control my food intake and I felt more relaxed. They did not have scales, so it was not possible for me to weigh myself. During that holiday I felt no pressure to achieve. For the first time in many years I liked having a holiday. I became interested in Asian culture, which was so different from my own. My self-esteem increased because of all the new experiences. When I came home after that holiday I was afraid to relapse into my old pattern of strict rules and rituals, but the need to do that had become much less. I discovered that my weight is quite stable, even when I eat a little more or less on some days. I am much more relaxed about my weight and no longer obsessed by food and calories.'

Being Able to Listen to Feelings of Hunger and Satiety

In the first period of extreme dieting, patients struggle to refrain from eating when they feel hungry, but when they succeed they get strong feelings of control and self-respect. The longer they are able to withstand their feelings of hunger, the stronger and more successful they feel. Eating disorder patients train themselves to ignore their feelings of hunger, fatigue and cold. They feel strong when they are able to ignore all the negative consequences of extreme dieting and starvation. They manage not to listen to the sensations of their body and to dissociate between their body and mind. To recover from their eating disorder, it is important that they learn to listen to physical sensations: feelings of hunger or satiety, being tired or feeling cold.

LINDA: 'In the therapy I had to learn to listen to my feelings of hunger and satiety. For many years I never ate enough and did not know any more when I had eaten enough and my stomach was full. I only regulated my food intake in a cognitive way by counting calories. I really had to overcome my fear when the dietician asked me to eat until I felt that my stomach was full.'

It is not only anorectic but also bulimic patients who have to learn when they feel physically hungry or satisfied. They often ignore their feelings of hunger until the stress has become so high that they need to have a binge. During a binge, they ignore all sensation of satiety and can only stop when they are completely exhausted or when they feel that their stomach may burst. An important goal for bulimic patients is to learn to listen to their sensations of hunger and satiety. They have to learn to eat when they are hungry and to stop when they feel that their stomach is full. They should also learn to distinguish between physical hunger and emotional hunger and to cope with negative emotions and stress.

MYRA: 'When I had a binge I swallowed my food without chewing and tasting it. I could only stop when my stomach felt extremely full, which was very painful. In the clinic I had to eat very slowly, taste my food carefully and chew it several times. In the first days I often felt an extreme need to have a binge, but after some weeks I had learned to eat much more slowly and with more attention. Mindful eating was very helpful for me. Now I can enjoy the taste of food and pay attention to my feelings of hunger and satiety. That greatly helped me to reduce my binges.'

LISETTE: 'During a binge I did not taste and chew, but just swallowed everything I pushed into my mouth. I ate very impulsively and could not enjoy the taste of food. In the treatment I had to sit at a table during a meal, eat slowly and taste and chew my food before swallowing. This was very helpful in changing my eating behaviour. Now I am so happy that I learned to eat in a normal way and appreciate taste. I can really enjoy my meals.'

Becoming sensitive to feelings of satiety takes much time and training.

ELLEN: 'I had bulimia for many years and had no idea anymore when I had eaten enough and when I felt satisfied. I did not feel satisfied after three slices of bread, not after five, and not even after eight or ten. I always felt I could just go on eating until my stomach burst. Each day I had to struggle not to have a binge. But I really wanted to win this fight. It took me several months, in which I had to learn to eat regularly and to eat normal amounts of food, before the feelings of appetite and satiety slowly returned. That was a great experience for me, because it meant that my body functioned again in a healthy way and could tell me when I needed food or when I had had enough.'

A useful therapy to for patients to become more connected with the sensations of their body is a body-focused therapy, in which patients have to explore their physical sensations. This therapy helps patients become more sensitive to all kinds of physical sensations and to express what they feel: tiredness, stress, cold or warmth, and hunger or contentment. A useful strategy to start with is to make patients more sensitive to the temperature of water.

> CLAES: 'I learned to pay more attention to all kinds of sensations in my skin. The therapist asked me to put my hands in a tub of water and to explore when the temperature of the water was too cold, too warm, or felt right for my skin. I learned to feel the sensation of my skin, which I had ignored for many years because I did not want to feel my body. Later on I had to practice with my feet. And finally I had to explore my physical feelings when taking a shower.'

Eating disorder patients often have problems with their respiration. Becoming more sensitive to the way they breathe can make them more relaxed:

> JOYCE: 'At the serious stage of my anorexia I felt completely disconnected from my body. In the therapy I started to pay attention to my breathing, which was very superficial and limited to the upper part of my body. In was told to breathe with my abdomen. That was very difficult for me, because it felt as if my stomach became round and fat, while I had always trained myself to keep it as flat as possible. But I learned that breathing with your abdomen has nothing to do with becoming fat, but only with the amount of fresh air in my lungs. When I practiced this deeper respiration I felt much more relaxed.'

Developing a Positive Body Attitude

Eating disorder patients focus only on the negative aspects of their body and often ignore the positive sides. They are very critical of anything which is not perfect in their eyes. It is important that they develop a more positive body attitude and learn to focus on the positive aspects of their body. A helpful strategy is to explore whether their cognitions about their body are right and fair.

> BEA: 'I thought my bum was very fat and was always afraid that others might notice it. My negative view of my behind started when I bought a pair of tight jeans and one of my friends said: "So, now everybody can admire your bum". Although he just wanted to make a compliment I saw his comment as negative, because I thought it meant that everybody could see how big my bum was. The consequence was that I did not want to wear those jeans before I had lost some weight and

my behind had become a bit smaller. I started to diet in an excessive way and developed anorexia. I became so emaciated that my jeans became too wide. But I had already become so obsessed by losing weight that I was unable to stop dieting. Finally my bottom had shrunk so much that it was painful to sit, so I needed a pillow. I always felt cold, so I wore many clothes, even in summer. Finally I realized that I had to change my life, and found a good therapist. She asked why I had started to diet. She showed me how I always had negative and critical thoughts about myself and my body. I had to learn to look at the positive aspects of my body. At the beginning of this treatment I was unable to see any positive sides to my body; I always looked at my bum and stomach and thought they were too fat. But the therapist taught me to look at my hair, eyes, the colour of my skin, etcetera. I learned to evaluate my body in a much more positive way and not to focus only on the negative parts. I am no longer obsessed by the negative aspects of my body and see them as parts of my body which belong to me and are necessary for adequate functioning. My body no longer has to be perfect, but it is OK as it is.'

Psycho-education about the way the human body functions is very important in the treatment of eating disorders.

CATHY: 'In the therapy I learned that it was very important to have some fat under my skin. A thin layer of fat protects you from feeling cold and functions as a pillow when you sit, so that you do not sit on your bones, because that is very painful. I learned to see my body in a more positive way and I feel much better now. Because of severe emaciation my body was in a very bad condition and I had all kinds of physical problems. After my treatment I feel much better and stronger, not only physically but also mentally. I never again want to diet and to suffer so much from all the negative consequences of my eating disorder.'

YVETTE: 'I wished that I had learned much earlier that it is normal for women to have a stomach which is not completely flat. I was always looking at pictures in magazines of women who had a totally flat stomach, and I wanted to look the same. Although I lost much weight my stomach never became really flat. Now I am glad that it is a little rounded. That is normal for women, and people see it as nice and feminine. I am much more satisfied with my appearance and I can really accept my figure.'

MARY: 'When my weight increased it was very difficult for me to accept that. I thought that everybody could see that I had become overweight and I saw my figure as ugly and fat. Because of this negative body image my therapist asked me to write a positive comment about my body in my notebook every day. Every week I had to show her my diary and I learned to focus more on all the positive aspects of my body.'

Assignment: Focus on positive aspects of your body

Most eating disorder patients focus only on the negative aspects of their body and ignore the positive sides. To develop a more positive body attitude, it is important to concentrate on the positive aspects. In the following list, we ask you to circle all those aspects of your body which are OK.

1. hair	11. neck	21. upper back
2. forehead	12. shoulder	22. lower back
3. eyebrows	13. upper arms	23. bum
4. eyes	14. lower arms	24. thighs
5. eyelashes	15. hands	25. knees
6. nose	16. fingers	26. calves
7. ears	17. nails	27. ankles
8. chin	18. torso	28. feet
9. teeth	19. breasts	29. toes
10. skin of your face	20. waist	30. toenails

How many body parts did you encircle?
Now make a short list of those parts of your body which you like.
Focus on these positive parts every day.

Assignment: Positive body evaluation

In this assignment, you learn to evaluate your body in a more positive way and to pay your body compliments. The positive evaluation should be directed not only at your body appearance but can also focus on the function of your body. For example: 'I like my hair and my eyes. Today I went for a very nice walk with our dog and that was real fun.'

Developing a positive body attitude does not mean that you have to be completely satisfied with all aspects of your body. The aim is to develop a general feeling of accepting yourself and your body, even those aspects which might not be as perfect as you would want.

You should write at least three positive things about your body in your notebook every day.

Monday:
1. ....
2. ....
3. ....

Tuesday:
1. ....
2. ....
3. ....

Wednesday:

1. ....
2. ....
3. ....

Thursday:

1. ....
2. ....
3. ....

Friday:

1. ....
2. ....
3. ....

Saturday:

1. ....
2. ....
3. ....

Sunday:

1. ....
2. ....
3. ....

WENDELA: 'By doing this assignment I learned to see myself as "good enough" and to accept my body as it is. I no longer look only at all those negative aspects, but focus much more on the positive aspects of my body. Although I will never become a real beauty I feel that my body is OK and fine.'

Learning Defence Strategies against Teasing

A negative view of their body, figure and weight is one of the core problems for eating disorder patients. Many former patients related that they were teased about their figure in the period before they started to diet.

JUDY: 'I already disliked my body long before I started to diet. I was ashamed of my legs, which were very sturdy. In primary school I was teased by girls who yelled at me that I was ugly and refused to play with me. After that experience my view of my body became even more negative. I decided to change my appearance in order to be more accepted by my class mates.'

In her diary, Natascha van Weezel (2006) writes that she was harassed by her school mates, who called her *fatty*, *bacon* or *pig*. This had a very negative impact on her body and self-evaluation.

NATASCHA: 'I internalized those words, "fatty", "bacon" and "pig" and even used them on myself when I ate too much.'

The consequences of being teased about your figure are that you feel very bad about your body. In the treatment, it is important to analyse which experiences have contributed to patients' negative body evaluation and to teach them strategies to defend themselves against negative comments of others.

LINDA: 'My therapist asked me when I had started to hate my body, and I felt ashamed to tell her what happened to me and what my schoolmates had said to me. The therapist asked me how I felt about my body when I heard those words, and how fair and right I thought they actually were. Although I was a little plump at the time, I surely was not fat like a pig. But being called "fatty" and "piggy" made me feel very bad about my body and I hated my figure. My therapist taught me to defend myself against these negative comments. Although the teasing happened many years ago it helped me to defend myself now. My therapist asked me to write a letter to the bullies and to make clear that teasing is not fair. This helped me to feel much better and stronger, even when that letter was never sent. Instead of internalising all the negative words I learned to defend myself much better. Although it was a shameful experience to tell my therapist about my being teased at school I was very glad that I learned strategies to defend myself.'

Assignment: Defence against teasing

Here are some questions about being teased about your body, figure or weight. You can write your answers in your diary or notebook.

Have you been teased about your body, weight or figure?

If yes, please answer the following questions:

1.   What words were used by the people who teased you?
2.   How right were these words?
3.   How fair were these words?
4.   Why might they have said that?
5.   What were your feelings at that moment?
6.   What was your reaction at that moment?

7. What would you say now?
8. Write your reaction in a letter to the persons who teased you (you do not have to actually send it).
9. Whom could you ask for help and support if you were teased again?
10. How would you react now if you were teased?

Here are Jessica's answers:

1. The words they used were: *fatty, piggy, Billy Bunter* and so on.
2. These words were not at all right; I was only slightly overweight.
3. Teasing is always unfair.
4. Reasons for teasing might have been that they are stupid and did not think about the meaning of these words, and they did not like me.
5. At that moment I felt very ashamed.
6. I tried to hide my body as much as possible.
7. Now I would say that they are wrong, and I would become very angry.
8. I would write that they showed a lot of disrespect. I cannot accept being called fatty, piggy or paunch.
9. I would talk about the bullying with my parents and best friend.
10. Now I would immediately ask for help and defend myself much better.

Losing the Urge to Diet

For patients to recover from an eating disorder, their urge to diet has to be reduced. Full recovery from an eating disorder implies that the patient no longer feels the need to diet.

> ADINA: 'I was always very sensitive about my weight, which was closely linked to my self-esteem: the higher my weight the lower my self-esteem, and vice versa. In the therapy I learned that my view of my weight had much to do with my feelings about myself. When everything was fine I felt that my weight was OK. But when I felt bad about myself my body felt fat. Feeling fat had nothing to do with my real weight, but everything with a negative self-evaluation. I learned that the way I felt about myself was "translated" into negative feelings about my body. In the therapy I had to analyse why I felt bad, and what I could do to feel better. I learned to develop better strategies than dieting: when I feel alone I can phone a friend; when I feel angry I can write in my diary why I am so angry. I learned many strategies to cope with my negative feelings. Although negative feelings are still "translated" into the feeling that my body is too fat, I now no longer start a diet, but use more effective strategies to reduce my negative feelings.'

For many former patients, psycho-education about the relation between negative emotions and feeling fat was very important. They have to learn that their emotions have become closely related to their body evaluation. Feeling fat is not an objective evaluation but a very subjective experience in which all kinds of negative emotions are expressed. Feeling fat is not the same as being overweight; it is closely associated with negative feelings and implies that you feel bad. When you feel bad, it is important to explore why you feel bad and to develop strategies to improve your emotions in order to feel better.

When you feel bad, dieting will not help you, as becomes clear from the experiences of Grace and Jeannet.

GRACE: 'For many years I felt fat, even when I dieted in an extreme way and my weight had become quite low. I realized that something was wrong with my strategy, because dieting did not help me to feel less fat and bad. In the therapy I learned that my mind makes the following short-cut: "feeling bad is feeling fat, and feeling fat means that I have to start a diet to lose weight". In the treatment I first had to analyse what situation it was that gave me bad feelings about myself and my body. I learned that it is not bad to have negative feelings, and feeling bad is not the same as being fat. I learned other strategies to improve my feelings and emotions, such as writing in my diary how I felt and why I felt that way. I also had to explore strategies for feeling better, such as mailing or phoning a friend. Analyzing my feelings and emotions was very helpful and I often felt relieved. My brains no longer translate negative emotions into feeling too fat.'

JEANNET: 'Unfortunately my feelings about my figure are still my weakest point. As soon as I feel negative, bored, or insecure I feel fat. I really feel fat and am convinced that I have to go on a diet. The feeling that I am fat is very strong, even when there is no objective reason for it, because my weight is normal. But when somebody criticizes me I immediately feel fat. So I translate my bad feelings into the feeling that I am too fat, because being fat is associated with all kinds of negative emotions and cognitions. I learned that feeling fat just means that I feel bad, sad or negative. Instead of starting a diet I now have to admit that is not bad to have negative feelings. Everybody has them. When I feel bad I first have to analyse which situation gave me those feelings. The second step is how to feel better without starting a diet. This strategy is very useful for me. I learned that I can change my negative feelings by using other strategies than extreme dieting.'

Assignment: Strategies to feel better

You can note here some strategies which make you feel better without dieting, for example, phoning a friend, taking a short walk, writing about your emotions in your diary, taking a shower or bath and so on. Make a list of strategies which may help you when you feel bad.

1. ....
2. ....
3. ....
4. ....
5. ....
Etc. ....

Questionnaire about a better body attitude

In the following questionnaire, you can indicate whether your body attitude has improved.

You can answer 1=no, 2=a little, 3=somewhat, 4=yes, 5=very high

1.	I no longer feel too fat	1	2	3	4	5
2.	I have a more positive body attitude	1	2	3	4	5
3.	I have learned to accept my appearance	1	2	3	4	5
4.	I do not diet anymore	1	2	3	4	5
5.	I am no longer obsessed by food and weight	1	2	3	4	5
6.	I am more satisfied with my body	1	2	3	4	5

Other aspects of improving my body attitude are:

7. 1   2   3   4   5
8. 1   2   3   4   5
9. 1   2   3   4   5
10. 1   2   3   4   5

If you answered some questions with 1, 2 or 3, you can discuss your answers with your therapist, so that these areas can be taken into account and receive extra attention in the treatment. If you answered some questions with a 4 or 5, you have improved and try to continue in the same manner.

Summary

In this chapter, recovered patients reported how they developed a more positive body attitude and no longer felt fat. They learned to accept their body with all its positive and negative aspects. Even when they sometimes feel that their weight has increased, they realize that dieting is not the solution to these negative feelings. They have learned alternative strategies for coping with negative emotions and are able to resist the pressure to be thin. They have learned to be more sensitive to the physical sensations of hunger and satiety. Psycho-education, cognitive therapy and body-focused therapy are very useful in helping patients to change distorted ideas about body, food and weight. They learn to focus on the positive aspects of their body. They are no longer obsessed with food and weight and are able to eat in a more relaxed way.

7

Physical Recovery

Introduction

Physical recovery from eating disorders focuses on regaining a normal weight. However, for anorectic patients a low weight is often not the most important problem. They suffer more from lack of energy and tiredness, insufficient sleep, damage to their teeth, dry skin, brittle nails and hair loss. The motivation to remedy these physical consequences of their eating disorder is often higher than the motivation to gain weight. Moreover, patients' fear of gaining weight is often very high, because they fear to lose control over their food intake and body. However, in order for their physical complaints to be cured, it is necessary that they eat more and gain weight.

In this chapter, the most important aspects of physical recovery are described, such as feeling energetic, maintaining a healthy and stable weight, normalizing hormone production and body temperature, normalizing heartbeat and pulse, overcoming constipation and bowel problems, getting enough sleep and having healthy teeth, nails and hair. How did former patients recover from the physical consequences of their eating disorder?

Normal and Stable Weight

For anorectic patients, weight recovery is very difficult, because their self-evaluation is closely linked to their weight. They have indoctrinated themselves for years with the dogma that 'losing weight is good and gaining weight is bad.' Weight loss gives them feelings of control and self-respect: 'This is

Recovery from Eating Disorders: A Guide for Clinicians and Their Clients,
First Edition. Greta Noordenbos.
© 2013 John Wiley & Sons, Ltd. Published 2013 by John Wiley & Sons, Ltd.

what I am capable of, this shows that I am strong and have control over my food intake and body.' For eating disorder patients, gaining weight is strongly related to their psychological self-evaluation and body experience. Gaining weight is seen as failure and as losing self-respect and control over their lives.

An important question is whether treatment should start by focusing on weight gain or by improving self-esteem, or should combine weight increase with developing more self-esteem.

However, in case of severe starvation, weight decreases to such an extent that patients are no longer able to think clearly and to reflect on their behaviour, thoughts and emotions, which makes psychotherapy very difficult at that stage. For such patients, increased food intake and gaining weight is an important condition for psychological improvement.

What do recovered patients say about their experiences with gaining weight?

AMY: 'I had become very emaciated and always had to sit on a pillow. I was extremely exhausted and depressed. In the end my parents decided to send me to a hospital. That was terrible for me because I was afraid to lose the control over my life. However, I realised that I was not able to change my eating behaviour and felt very weak. I was so tired and depressed, and I had so much pain and suffered from all kinds of physical problems. I realised that I could not continue my life if I remained greatly underweight. But when the nurses started the tube feeding I felt that I lost the last bit of control over my life. However, after an extremely difficult period of supplementary feeding my weight increased slowly and I felt a little better. I had a bit more energy and could think more clearly. And although my "feelings" said "no" to increasing weight, my "cognition" said that this might be the only way to save my life. For me it was very important that during the period of tube feeding attention was paid not only to my body, but also to my emotions. Every day a psychologist came to talk to me. She asked how I felt and she understood how difficult and frightening this experience was for me. She assured me that after some weeks I would feel better and less depressed. My parents were also very supportive. Finally I felt I was getting out of a deep pit. Now I really cannot understand any more how I could have fallen so low. I never want to go back to that awful situation in which I needed tube feeding. If my parents had not sent me to that hospital I would not have survived and might have died.'

Amy's story makes it clear that increasing food intake and gaining weight is a difficult experience, but it is an important condition for physical and psychological recovery. During the stage of weight increase, the patient needs emotional support from family and a professional therapist. Recovered patients can also offer support, because they have gone through the same process and can serve as relevant role models.

Regular Periods

When the female body does not get enough food and loses weight drastically, periods become irregular. Amenorrhea is found not only in anorectic women but also in bulimic patients who vomit often or use laxatives. When the female body is undernourished, it no longer produces enough hormones to activate monthly periods. The menses start again only when patients eat enough and gain weight. For most eating disorder patients, however, having regular periods is not their first priority. It is important for them that attention is paid not only to the physical aspects of having periods, but also to their body attitude, as illustrated by the experiences of recovered patients.

> CORINE: 'My general practitioner advised me that it was important that my periods should become regular again. But having a regular menstruation was not motivating for me, because I had had very negative experiences with my periods, which always started with a headache, stomach ache and a bloated feeling. I really hated my periods. For me it was a relief that they stayed away, and I did my best to keep my weight low.'

> FENNY: 'The return of my periods was quite difficult for me. Of course I knew that this was a sign that you have a healthy female body, but for long time I had very negative feelings about my menstruation: I felt bloated and dirty. Fortunately I had a very kind therapist who told me that having periods is a sign that your body functions in a healthy way. That helped me to realize that menstruation is part of my body.'

Some patients are motivated to get back to having regular menses when they want to become pregnant. Information about the relation between food, weight and monthly periods is helpful to motivate them to eat more and to gain weight.

> ODILE: 'For a long time I retained a very low weight as I did not want to have periods, because I had very negative feelings about my menstruation. But recently some of my friends became pregnant and had babies. When I saw their lovely babies I really wanted to have one myself. Having children was an important part of my future. That helped me to become motivated towards gaining weight. However, it took a long time before I got pregnant. I really worried about the consequences of my extreme slimming regime and abuse of laxatives. I was afraid that my eating disorder had damaged my body so that I could not become pregnant. That helped me to become motivated to eat healthy food and to regain a normal weight. Of course I was very glad when I finally got pregnant. Now I am very proud of my daughter and would never have missed that experience.'

Normal Body Temperature

Because of being severely underweight, the body temperature of anorectic patients is very low. They lose all fat under their skin and feel very cold. When the body does not get enough energy, all physical processes slow down in order to protect the central organs in the body, causing the hands and feet to become red or blue due to reduced blood circulation. A low body temperature is very uncomfortable for anorectic patients.

ARNOLD: 'I was always cold, and although I liked swimming I was not able to swim any more because the water was too cold for me. When I went to school I wore lots of warm clothes so that I was less cold and others could not see my figure. My hands became red and I tried to hide them in long sleeves. I preferred to sit next to the central heating and even then I felt cold. It is strange that during my anorexia I never realised that this was a consequence of my reduced food intake and low weight. In the clinic they told me that a low temperature and cold hands and feet are a consequence of starvation. I had to eat more, and slowly developed more fat under my skin so that my body temperature rose and I was cold less often. For me it was very rewarding that after several months of gaining weight I was able go to the swimming pool and swim without trembling and feeling extremely cold.'

TATJANA: 'In the clinic for eating disorders I was made to eat more. Slowly my weight increased, as well as my body temperature. I did not have to wear so many clothes to keep a comfortable body temperature. At the end of the treatment we went to a swimming pool with quite warm water. Although I was very afraid to show my body in a swimsuit, it was a nice experience. Swimming had always been my favourite sport. I experienced how important it is to have a thin layer of fat under my skin. I had always seen fat as bad and ugly, and now I realized how important it is to have some fat under my skin. I do not feel cold any more, and it does not hurt when I sit or lie down.'

Normal Heartbeat and Pulse

As a consequence of starvation, the heartbeat and pulse become slower, while frequent vomiting and abuse of laxatives cause an irregular heartbeat. The heart is a muscle which can function only when there are enough electrolytes in the body. Frequent vomiting and abuse of laxatives can be life-threatening (Tenwolde, 2000). Anorectic patients consume very few calories because they are afraid of gaining weight, while bulimic patients vomit and use laxatives to get rid of all the calories they consume during their binges. They are often unaware that their eating habits can have severe consequences for their heart. According to Tenwolde (2000), 75% of anorectic patients have chest pains or complaints comparable to angina pectoris, or experience heart palpitation, dizzy spells and fainting. These complaints are the consequence of malnutrition and an extremely low weight, which reduces the number and length of muscular tissues, especially in the left ventricle of the heart. This can lead to lack of oxygen, reduced power of the heart muscle, a reduced volume of the heart ventricles and a decrease in the heart's pumping capacity or an irregular heartbeat.

Severe malnutrition can also result in reduced blood pressure and a lower heartbeat which can become even lower than 40 per minute. Because of reduced blood pressure, anorectic patients often feel dizzy and run the risk of fainting (Tenwolde, 2000).

Anorectic patients are in danger of dying because of heart dysfunction. Tube feeding, however, has to be done very carefully and slowly. When anorectic patients receive too much food in a short period of time, their hearts might not able to cope with these quantities of food. In case of tube feeding, medical care is necessary. For eating disorder patients, a reduced level of potassium and irregular heartbeat can become critically dangerous and may even lead to instant death. This is one of the main causes of death in bulimic patients.

CHRISTINA: 'When I read about all the negative effects my eating behaviour could have on my heart I really became very scared. This motivated me to change my food intake, and stop my vomiting and abuse of laxatives.'

CAROLINE: 'I got very scared when I my heart rhythm became severely disturbed. I was really afraid that I would die. I never thought that bulimia might be life-threatening. I felt alarmed and went to my GP, and told him about my eating problem. He referred me to a cardiologist, and to a clinic for eating disorders to help me reduce my binges and purging. For the first time I was motivated to change my eating behaviour, although it was not easy to cut back on my binging and purging. But I realised that I damaged my body if I did not change. Sometimes I had a nightmare and dreamed that my heart stopped beating. I really wanted to be rid of the binges, vomiting and laxative abuse. And I succeeded! Now I am so glad when I wake up and feel my heart beating regularly.'

No Anaemia

According to Tenwolde (2000), 30% of patients with anorexia and bulimia nervosa develop anaemia. The most important causes of anaemia are a defective production of bone marrow, lack of iron and lack of vitamins B12 and B1.

MARY: 'During the years when I had anaemia I had a severe iron deficiency and I looked very pale. When I was admitted into the clinic for eating disorders I was given important information about food by a dietician. She told me which nutrients my body needs to be able to function in a healthy way. This information was very revealing, because I had always thought that the intake of fat was unhealthy and calories were bad. I realised that I had neglected my body for many years. I learned that my body functions as a complex factory, and needs a diversity of food which can be transformed into nutrients for all parts of my body.'

ELISA: 'The doctor in the clinic explained to us which foods are necessary for a healthy body. In the first period of my treatment I received vitamins, and also capsules with iron and fish oil. The doctor told me that these nutrients are important for my brain and blood vessels. Before my treatment I would never have taken fish oil, because I was really afraid of eating fat. But when I started to eat those capsules I felt much better. The dietician told us about all kinds of food which are necessary to keep your body in a good condition. So I learned that most of the nutrients you need can be found in healthy and diverse food, such as vegetables, beans, nuts, and all kinds of fruit.'

No Constipation

Eating disorders patients who do not eat enough, or vomit and use laxatives, often have problems with their bowels. Their bowels become *lazy* from lack of stimulation when patients do not eat enough, or because laxatives stimulate the bowels in an artificial way. When patients do not use laxatives, they suffer from severe constipation and take even more laxatives. Finally, they get into a vicious circle, as becomes clear from Arjanne's account:

ARJANNE: 'When I started to diet I wanted to eat as little as possible in order to lose weight in a short time. Then I read that laxatives could prevent the food from being transformed into sugar in your intestines. I started with a few laxatives but gradually I needed more. Then I got the idea to take some laxatives before I started to eat. I thought that laxatives might reduce my feelings of hunger, and the food would leave my body as soon as possible. The consequence was severe pain in my stomach and bowels. Sometimes when I was on the toilet, I felt as if I was pushing out my intestines, because I had hardly any food in my body. That was terrible but I could not change my behaviour, because as soon as I reduced the number of laxatives. I started to suffer from constipation. One day my mother found me lying on the floor with extreme pain in my stomach. She immediately got a doctor, who phoned an ambulance to take me to the hospital. That was terrible, but this intervention saved my life. After some awful weeks in which I was not allowed to take any laxatives my bowels became reactivated. I learned that my body was able to recover. That for me was a very important step in the way to recovery.'

No Problems with Bowels and Stomach

When the bowels are not activated by regular food intake, the peristaltic movements reduce. If laxatives are used, the bowels are only activated in an artificial way. During supplementary feeding, the bowels have to be activated by gradually increasing food intake. In the first period of this new regime, eating disorder patients soon feel *full* or bloated even after a small amount of food. To reduce their constipation, the consumption of fibres and vegetables and drinking enough water can be helpful.

Binges can have serious consequences, and in severe cases result in a rupture of the stomach (Tenwolde, 2000). Because of the life-threatening effects of a rupture of the stomach, hospitalization is necessary. Most stomach problems diminish with healthy food intake and regular meals. In case of more serious problems, it is necessary to consult a GP or a dietician. In order to recover from stomach pain, the patient should abstain from coffee, alcohol and spices.

No more Swollen Salivary Glands and Sore Throat

Frequent vomiting after a binge can lead to swollen salivary glands. This often irks bulimic patients as it makes their face broader.

> CHRISTA: 'I was very disappointed that when I lost weight my face became broader because of swollen salivary glands. That was a very bad effect of my frequent vomiting. In the clinic for eating disorders it was forbidden to vomit after a meal. That was very difficult for me, but the positive thing was that my face became normal again, although I was very afraid that I might become fat if I could not vomit. The reduction of the swelling of my glands stimulated me to reduce my binging and purging behaviour.'

Frequent vomiting has many negative consequences, such as dehydration, a sore and irritated throat, lack of saliva, dry lips and inflamed gums (Tenwolde, 2000). Bionda reports how bad these consequences were for her.

> BIONDA: 'Because I used many laxatives I lost a lot of fluids in my body. A positive effect was that my weight went down, but the price for this was high because of all the negative consequences. My mouth was very

dry and I had hardly any saliva, so that I needed to drink a lot of water during the day, especially when I wanted to eat something. It was very difficult to eat dry food such as a piece of bread. For that reason I only took liquid food such as yoghurt and pudding. But the worst consequence was that my face looked swollen. I really thought that everybody could see how bloated my face had become. When I gradually stopped using laxatives all these negative consequences disappeared. My salivary glands went back to normal, and my throat was no longer irritated. I am very happy that my face is a normal shape again.'

Because of frequent vomiting, bulimic patients can suffer from a sore throat:

GWEN: 'When I had bulimia I had an urgent need to vomit after a binge. I even put Q-tips or a toothbrush down my throat, which was quite dangerous. I had a very sore throat, and after vomiting I often felt dizzy and thought I would faint. But I could not stop vomiting because after a binge I felt extremely bad with all that food in my stomach. I panicked when I could not vomit. After vomiting there was a short period of relief, but that was soon followed by a sore throat and a dry mouth. So I finally decided not to vomit any more. After some weeks my throat was no longer painful and my mouth no longer so dry. That motivated me to continue with my process of recovery.'

Healthy Skin

Lack of food and liquids can result in a dry, pale skin. A pale skin can also be the consequence of anaemia, while a yellow-coloured skin can be the result of eating too many carrots (Tenwolde, 2000).

RACHEL: 'In pictures from my anorectic period you can clearly see that my skin had a strange yellow colour and looked old because it was very dry. In that period I ate mostly carrots and cucumber in order to reduce my calorie intake. In the clinic the dietician taught me to eat more and vary my food more. After some months my skin had a normal colour and was no longer so yellow, pale and dry. When I compare myself with how I was in my anorectic period I can clearly see the differences. My skin has a much better condition and colour. I realise now how important it is to eat enough, and varied, food.'

Healthy Teeth

Lack of food and frequent vomiting can result in bleeding gums and damaged teeth. Because of the erosion of the enamel, the back side of the teeth can become very thin, so that drinking very warm or very cold liquids is very painful. Sometimes the enamel becomes so thin that the dentine or pulpa comes to the surface, which is extremely painful. Sometimes the front teeth become shorter and very sharp (Tenwolde, 2000). Many eating disorder patients have bleeding or inflamed gums, which has severe consequences for their teeth.

> JOYCE: 'At a certain moment it was very painful when I tried to eat some-thing which had to be chewed, because my gums were severely inflamed. When I brushed my teeth my gums always started bleeding. After a period of frequent vomiting the enamel at the back side of my front teeth had become very thin so that it was very painful to eat or drink cold and warm food and fluids. For many years I did not drink warm tea or coffee, because that was too painful. I could only man-age lukewarm water or tea. I could not eat warm soup or drink hot chocolate either, although I liked those very much. One of the first tasks in my treatment programme was to go to the dentist, who com-pletely restored my teeth. Although I now have quite a few artificial teeth I am very glad that I am able to drink coffee and tea again with-out pain. During my treatment in the clinic I had to learn to eat and drink all kinds of "new" foods because I had not eaten these for sev-eral years. Now I am very happy that I can again have my favourite soup and hot chocolate. I advise eating disorder patients to go to a dentist as soon as they have any complaints regarding their teeth, because of all the negative effects of malnutrition and vomiting.'

To prevent severe problems with gums and teeth, the use of mouthwash is advised after vomiting. It is also important to consult a dentist as soon as possible.

> VICKY: 'Because of the lack of food and vitamins my gums were always red and bleeding, and very painful. I finally went to the dentist. That was rather late so he needed to take out some of my front teeth and molars. I felt terrible about that. Although I am very young I now have a dental plate with several false teeth. When I started to diet I never thought that this might be a consequence of my extreme slim-ming behaviour and weight loss. I wish I had known that before, because then I might have stopped vomiting at a much earlier stage.'

Enough Sleep

Many eating disorder patients do not get enough sleep during the night. Anorectic patients often feel hungry at night and cannot sleep because their stomach is empty. They constantly think about food and even dream about it. Another reason why they cannot sleep is that they have lost much weight and have hardly any fat under their skin. Lying with their knees together can be very painful.

Bulimic patients, too, often do not sleep enough. When they take many laxatives, they have stomach pain and have to go to the toilet frequently. If they did not eat enough during the daytime, or have vomited after a binge, they might feel hungry at night, which can trigger another binge. Their sleep pattern is completely disturbed and in the morning they still feel tired.

The most effective strategy to reduce sleeping problems is to have regular meals and enough food during the day, and not to vomit or use laxatives, so that patients will not feel hungry at night. As their weight increases, it is less painful for anorectic patients to lie in bed, because they develop some fat tissue between their skin and bones.

FATIMA: 'For many years I did not sleep well, so that I was very tired during daytime and could not concentrate on my school work. Although I was often very tired when I went to bed I always felt some pain in my stomach because it was empty. I always worried that I ate too much during the day so that I was already calculating the amount of calories I was allowed to eat the next day. It often dreamed about food, especially "forbidden" food. Because of my severe emaciation it was very difficult to find a position in which my knees or my back did not hurt. My skin had become very thin, and finally my parents bought some very soft blankets for me to lie on and a small blanket which I could have between my knees, because I could not have one knee over the other, that was too painful. When I was finally referred to the hospital and was forced to eat more, I could not sleep during the first week because I was so scared about all those calories in my body. It took some weeks before I was able to sleep better, because I was no longer extremely hungry during the night, and had developed a thin layer of fat under my skin so that lying in bed was less painful. Because I slept much better I could think more clearly and became less obsessed by food and weight. When I was allowed to leave the hospital I went to a clinic for eating disorders where I learned to eat more regularly. Now I feel much better. Each night I sleep seven to eight hours and I feel refreshed when I wake up. I can concentrate much better on my lessons, and already passed my first examination with good results.'

Enough Energy

One of the most frequent consequences of malnutrition is lack of energy. Eating disorder patients often feel tired and exhausted. Lack of sleep, frequent binges, vomiting and extreme exercising also contribute to lack of energy.

ROSALINDE: 'When I had severe anorexia I often felt extremely tired, even
after the smallest exertion. In order to lose weight I forced
myself to run long distances. Finally I had become very emaciated and was no longer able to exercise for any length of time.
I felt so weak that I sometimes fainted. That was terrible because
I wanted to be strong and tough. Sport and fitness were very
important for me, but the less I ate and the more weight I lost
the less energy I had. Although I felt like a rag doll I was very
scared to eat more and to gain weight.'

Although most eating disorder patients are highly motivated to gain more
energy, they are also scared of consuming more calories because they believe
calories make them fat. However, they have to abandon their dogma 'calorie = fat = bad', and have to learn that 'calorie = energy.'

HELENA: 'The dietician taught me how calories work in your body. I always
learned from magazines that calories make you fat, and when you
want to become very thin you need to reduce your calorie intake.
I never read that your body needs calories as fuel for all kinds of
physical processes such as breathing, walking, using your brains or
keeping your body warm. The dietician told me that the definition
of a calorie is the amount of energy necessary to heat water one
centigrade. The body needs enough calories in order to function in
a healthy way. Your weight will increase only when you eat more
calories than what your body uses.

When she asked what I ate she calculated that I did not get enough calories for heating my body, so that my body temperature was too low. I had
exhausted my body so that I often felt tired and could not concentrate on
school. My therapist taught me that it was very important to eat enough
calories, because that is an essential condition for a healthy body and
mind. Although her information was very relevant, it did take me some
time to abandon my strict dogmas that calories are fat and fat is bad. But
I actually experienced that more food gave me more energy. That was
very stimulating. Now I can go to school again and I am much better
able to concentrate. The idea that all calories make you fat is a total
misconception.'

Reduction of Osteoporosis

A damaging consequence of malnutrition is reduced bone density, or osteoporosis (Tenwolde, 2000). The consequences of osteoporosis are often not
felt in the first period of an eating disorder. However, in the long run bone

density may diminish. Osteoporosis increases the risk of bone fractures, a bent back or scoliosis, compression of the vertebrae and hernia because of a slipped disc. To turn back loss of bone density is very difficult. The best strategy to reduce these negative consequences is increased intake of food containing healthy nutrients (Tenwolde, 2000).

> NICKY: 'When I heard from my general practitioner that lack of food might result in osteoporosis I became very afraid, because I had seen the consequences of osteoporosis in my grandmother. When she became older she developed a bent back. When I heard that osteoporosis can be a consequence of anorexia nervosa, I really became motivated to eat more healthy and varied food. My GP gave me calcium to reduce the effect of my malnutrition.'

Questionnaire about physical recovery

In this questionnaire, you can indicate whether your physical condition has improved:

You can answer 1 = no, 2 = very little, 3 = somewhat, 4 = yes, 5 = very much

1.	I feel less tired	1	2	3	4	5
2.	I have more energy	1	2	3	4	5
3.	I feel more fit	1	2	3	4	5
4.	I have less constipation	1	2	3	4	5
5.	I have less bowel problems	1	2	3	4	5
6.	I feel less cold	1	2	3	4	5
7.	I feel less pain when I sit or lie down	1	2	3	4	5
8.	I have a better skin condition	1	2	3	4	5
9.	I have a better hair condition	1	2	3	4	5
10.	I have stronger nails	1	2	3	4	5
11.	I have stronger teeth	1	2	3	4	5
12.	I have less swollen salivary glands	1	2	3	4	5

Other physical problems which are reduced:

11.	....	1	2	3	4	5
12.	....	1	2	3	4	5
13.	....	1	2	3	4	5
14.	....	1	2	3	4	5

If you answered some questions with 1, 2 or 3, you can discuss your answers with your therapist, so that these areas can be taken into account and receive extra attention in the treatment. If you answered some questions with a 4 or 5, you have improved and try to continue in the same manner.

Summary

Many negative physical consequences of eating disorders disappear once intake of food and weight are normalized: the body temperature becomes normal and the production of hormones increases sufficiently for women to have regular periods. Problems such as low blood pressure and a slow heart-beat as well as disturbances of heart rhythm also diminish. Constipation and problems with bowel movements disappear after reduction of the intake of laxatives and diuretics. Most sleep disturbances also disappear when patients eat three regular and healthy meals a day with some snacks in-between and no longer have binges followed by purging and vomiting. The skin becomes less dry and pale, and hair and nails become stronger. However, not all physical consequences of an eating disorder disappear completely after weight increase and normalization of food intake. For damaged teeth, it is necessary to consult a dentist, and while osteoporosis cannot be turned back, the consequences can be reduced by eating enough nourishing food.

As the condition of eating disorder patients improves, most physical problems disappear. Their psychological condition also improves substantially: they can concentrate much better and feel less tired and depressed. The next chapter deals with the psychological improvement of recovered patients.

8

Developing More Self-Esteem

Introduction

For eating disorder patients, improving self-esteem and self-respect is very important in order to recover (Fodor, 1997; Reindl, 2001). Without this, the risk of relapse is very high (Bruch, 1978; Fennig, Fennig, & Roe, 2002; Strober, Freeman, & Morrell, 1997). In this chapter, recovered eating disorder patients describe how they developed more self-esteem and a better self-evaluation. They became less pleasing to others and learned to listen to their own feelings and emotions. They became less dependent on the approval of others and less afraid of rejection. It was very helpful for them to become more assertive and to dare to express their own opinions. Moreover, their perfectionism and fear of failure diminished, as well as their self-criticism. They became more compassionate towards themselves. Their sense of self was empowered and their self-respect improved substantially.

More Self-Esteem

For eating disorder patients, self-esteem is closely connected with weight and food intake. In the period just after they start to diet, they feel very proud of themselves. When the scales go down, their self-esteem increases, but when the scales show a higher weight, their self-esteem decreases.

EMMA: 'At the first stage of my eating disorder losing weight gave me much self-respect. The more weight I lost the higher my self-esteem. But

Recovery from Eating Disorders: A Guide for Clinicians and Their Clients,
First Edition. Greta Noordenbos.
© 2013 John Wiley & Sons, Ltd. Published 2013 by John Wiley & Sons, Ltd.

when I lost control over my eating behaviour and had binges, I lost not only the control over my food intake, but also my self-respect, which was strongly related to my control over food. To lose both control over food and my self-respect was terrible, a real nightmare.'

To increase patients' self-esteem, the positive support of a therapist and their family and friends is very important.

SUZY: 'I was only able to see positive aspects of myself when I met a therapist who accepted me as I was, even with my eating disorder. She believed in me before I could believe in myself. Without her constant support I would not have been able to recover. She was not afraid of my fear, sorrow or rage and that made it possible for me to accept all the negative feelings which I had suppressed and hidden deep in myself. This therapist supported me in developing my own qualities. She really helped me to build up more self-respect.'

Positive support from a therapist is very important if patients are to develop more self-esteem. They can learn to internalize the positive feedback of the therapist and look at themselves in a more positive way (Gilbert, 2010; Neff, 2011).

However, developing more self-respect is very difficult for patients if their parents are very critical. The consequence might be that they continuously hear their parents' comments in their heads:

CATHY: 'I had completely internalised my mother's critical comments. She called me an egoist and did not like my clothes and style of hair. Nothing I did was good enough, it could always be better. Even my friends were criticized. I was always up against her critical attitude. I even heard her critical comments when she just looked at me but said nothing. When I wanted to buy new clothes I already anticipated my mother's disapproval. Only when I met a therapist who gave me positive feedback did I manage to build a little more self-respect and begin to develop a more positive view of myself.'

In order to develop more self-esteem, it is not enough to receive more positive feedback. It is very important to empower oneself. Useful therapeutic strategies are cognitive behavioural therapy (CBT) (Fairburn, Cooper, & Shafran, 2003) or compassion-focused therapy (CFT) (Gilbert, 2010).

TALITA: 'An important part of the treatment was to develop more positive thoughts about myself and to build more self-esteem. One of the assignments I was given was that whenever I heard negative and criti-cal comments in my head I had to think about some positive aspects of myself. Each evening I had to write some positive and comforting things about myself in my diary. The first time I sat before my brand-new diary with the completely blank and empty pages, no positive thoughts came into my mind. The only thing I could think of was that I was bad and ugly. But I had to write something: at least one or two positive points. Each week I became better at noting down some positive aspects of myself, and after some months I had really learned to have more positive thoughts about myself. I was able to think: "OK, I could have done better at that examination, but I really have done my best." My self-image was no longer merely negative.'

Developing a better image of oneself takes much training but can be quite effective when patients focus each day on the positive experiences they have had.

JUDY: 'Each day I was able to note some positive aspects in my diary, even if they were minor details. For example "I was well-prepared for my presentation in school. I had a nice talk with a schoolmate. I phoned a friend and asked her to go with me to a film this weekend", etcetera. This positive way of thinking was very helpful for me. Before the therapy I always had very high standards for myself, and if I did not realise them I thought I had failed and I was very disappointed in myself. Now I have more compassion with myself and pay more attention to all those small and concrete things in my life which are OK and positive. My self-image is no longer negative and I am not so critical about myself. My self-respect has substantially improved.'

Assignment: Training positive thinking

The following assignment can help you develop more positive opinions about yourself. Every day, write down at least three positive things about yourself in your diary and make them very concrete. Here is an example:

LUCY: 'Today I was able to concentrate very well at school and did my best. I only made two small mistakes, but all other things went well. I had a very pleasant talk with a schoolmate. When I came home I helped my younger brother with his school work. I ate a healthy meal.'

What are your positive thoughts about yourself?

1. ....
2. ....
3. ....
4. ....
5. ....

Empowering Yourself

Low self-esteem and a negative self-evaluation are major problems in the period before the development of an eating disorder. Patients' insecurities make them very sensitive to the opinion and approval of others. They strongly focus on what they think other persons expect of them. However, because of their compliant and pleasing behaviour, they do not learn to listen to their own feelings and opinions. Debby is very clear about this process:

DEBBY: 'My mother was often very depressed, because she missed my father who died very young. I saw how much she suffered and tried to help her and to cheer her up whenever possible. When I looked at her face I could see when she felt depressed, and then I tried hard to cheer her up. I never told her anything about my own problems and sad feelings. I continuously tried to improve my mother's mood and was always thinking what I could to help her. But nobody asked me how I felt and what I wanted. In the long run I completely lost the feeling of having a "self" with its own feelings and needs.'

Although patients' self-esteem increases substantially in the first stage of dieting, this is only related to control over food and weight, not to other aspects of their lives. In the therapy, it is very important to discover what they really feel and want.

SARAH: 'In the therapy I had to learn what *I felt* and what *I wanted*, instead of trying to please others. This was very difficult for me because I really did not know what I felt and desired. Only very slowly did I learn to listen to my own feelings and explore my own wishes and needs. In the treatment I learned to express my own feelings and needs much better. I discovered that I had a "*self*" and no longer only had to do what others expected me to do. I was no longer focused on the expectations of others and no longer tried to comply with them. I learned to stand up for myself and no longer to sacrifice my own ideas. Of course I try to take into account what others want and feel, but I do not lose my "*self*" any more and am no longer always self-effacing.'

Become More Assertive

In the process of developing more self-esteem, it is important to become more assertive and to stand up for one's own wishes and opinions. For most eating disorder patients, this is very difficult, because they have often tried to please others and to comply with others' expectations, fearing that they might otherwise not be accepted or even be rejected. They are often afraid to defend themselves against the expectations of others.

ARINA: 'Standing up for myself was only possible when my feelings about myself became more positive and my self-esteem increased. I learned a lot from other people who were much more assertive than I was. I saw them as "models", and learned how I could stand up for myself without being afraid to be seen as egoistic, forward, or ignoring others. I always thought that when I stood up for myself others would not like me any more. In the therapy I learned to become more assertive. I experienced that when I made my own wishes and opinions clear, other people still accepted me.'

It is important to practice assertiveness by role-playing.

JOLANDA: 'In the treatment I had to learn to stand up for myself instead of thinking about what others thought of me. That was extremely difficult for me, because I always tried to please others and to find out what they liked or thought. What helped me very much was that I had the opportunity to practice this assertive behaviour via role-playing with other patients. My therapist explained to me that when you defend yourself you need to take yourself seriously, but this does not imply a negative attitude towards others. Other people also take themselves seriously, why should I not do the same? It was very important that my therapist told me that everybody has their own opinions, and that it is important to listen to your own opinions and to accept that people can have different views. Why not respect my own opinion?'

WILLIAM: 'I had to learn to express *my own feelings and opinions* instead of always listening to the opinions and expectations of others. Only after many role-playing sessions was I prepared to become more assertive in real-life situations. I found that having a different opinion did not immediately imply being rejected by others. That felt very good, and I learned to be assertive not only in the treatment but also in contacts with family and friends. Before my treatment I always set aside my own wishes and opinions, because I was so afraid that others would criticise me. Now I can express my own feelings and opinions and defend them.'

In order to learn to become more assertive and to stand up for oneself, it is necessary to train in all kinds of different situations. Role-playing is very helpful to become more assertive.

Assignment: Becoming more assertive

In this assignment, we ask you to describe what you would say in the following situations. You can discuss your answers with your therapist and so learn to become more assertive.

1. You are in a shop and want to buy a nice green dress, but your friend says that red is a better colour for you. What do you say to your friend? My answer is ....

2. A schoolmate asks to borrow the book you are reading. However, this is not your own book, because you yourself borrowed it from a friend and promised her to return it as soon as possible. You tell your schoolmate this, but she says that she can read very fast and only needs one day to read the book. What is your reaction?
    ....

3. Make some assignments for situations which are important for you. What do you want to do? How can you defend yourself? What will you say when others don't agree with your opinion?
    ....
    ....

Less Emphasis on Pleasing others

People who develop an eating disorder are often very insecure about themselves and dependent on the approval of others. Therefore, they often try to please others and to comply with others' expectations. This is why the famous author Jane Fonda labels an eating disorder the *disease to please*.

MIRJAM: 'Before I developed my eating disorder I was very compliant and tried to do what others expected me to do. I was afraid they would criticize me, and then feel completely rejected. But in the therapy I learned to express my own wishes, needs and opinions. Now I am much less dependent on the opinion of others. Of course I still like to get positive reactions or compliments from others, but first of all I try to make clear what I really want or think.'

ELISA: 'In the treatment I have become much less dependent on the opinions of others and less afraid to be criticized. If somebody criticizes me I first ask myself whether those remarks are correct, and if not I defend my own opinion. I no longer need others' approval for everything I do, and I am not afraid to do what is important for myself. That has made a huge difference in my life and feels very good. Looking back on the period before my eating disorder I really cannot understand why I was so compliant and always tried to please others. Now I have my own opinions and wishes and dare to express them, even if others do not agree.'

In the treatment, it is important for patients to learn to make a difference between helpful criticism and destructive criticism. Helpful criticism can be seen as advice to help you to improve your behaviour. Destructive criticism, however, is only negative and you cannot learn from it. You just learn to feel bad about yourself. Cognitive therapy can be very useful to learn to distinguish between helpful and destructive criticism.

GWEN: 'Before my eating disorder I was extremely dependent on the opinion of others and I was very sensitive to what they thought about me. I was very afraid that they did not like me and would criticise me. In the treatment I learned to analyse what they said and to differentiate between constructive and merely destructive criticism. When the critical remarks are constructive I no longer have the feeling that I am failing, and I try to analyse what I can learn from it. With destructive criticism I learned not to pay any attention. I have become much less dependent on others and feel more secure about my own opinions.'

KATHY: 'Before my anorexia my parents were carping at me a lot. If I did not agree with their critical remarks they told me that I could not cope with criticism. Their comments made me very insecure. In the clinic for eating disorders I learned to become less insecure about myself. I learned that I should try and understand the intention of the person who criticised me. When the intention is OK I can learn from the critical remarks and no longer feel completely rejected by that person. My self-respect and self-esteem have become much stronger.'

Having Less Fear of Rejection

Eating disorder patients are very sensitive to negative and critical remarks from others. Because of their fear of rejection, they try very hard to prevent any negative and critical comments. Their complying and pleasing behaviour is strongly related to their fear of not being accepted by others. In the treatment, it is very important to reduce this fear.

FARIDA: 'When I was a child I was always very afraid of other people criticizing me. If somebody did not agree with what I said I saw that as criticism of my whole person and felt completely rejected. I always thought that when other people criticized me they no longer liked me. I found that a frightening thought. I always did my best to prevent others from criticizing me. In the therapy, however, I learned that when somebody criticizes you this does not mean that they reject you as a person. They only criticize some aspects of your behaviour. Moreover, you do not have to agree with them. I have acquired much more self-respect and am no longer so dependent on the opinion others have of me.'

GRACE: 'In the therapy I learned that not everybody has to like me or to be my friend. Now I feel much more relaxed in relationships and try to find out whether I like somebody or not. Before my eating disorder I felt completely rejected when somebody did not like me. Now I am glad that I can think about relationships in a more realistic way. Not everybody has to like me and not all criticism means that you are rejected by that person. I have much more self-respect.'

Assignment: Defending yourself against critical comments

A helpful assignment to reduce your fear of criticism from and rejection by others is to analyse what they say to you and what their intentions are. First write down what kind of critical or negative remarks people have made in your diary. Then analyse whether the remarks were really meant to criticize you or were just a slip of the tongue. If the remarks were actually critical, it can be helpful to find out whether that critics did have a point, so that you can learn from their comments. However, if you feel that the criticism was unfair and merely destructive, it is important that you learn to defend yourself. It can be helpful to see yourself as a lawyer defending yourself. The next step is to write your own defence. What arguments can you make? When you train yourself to stand up for yourself, you will become much stronger and less afraid of the critical remarks of others.

As an example, refer to Ben's assignment in the following:

My teacher's critical remark was: 'You are always late!'
My answer is: 'That is not correct, because most days I was on time. Last week, however, I was late because the bus was delayed, so that was not my fault. Today I came in late because I missed the bus: that was my own fault and I will try not to let that happen again. It is, however, not fair to say that I am *always* late.'

Here you can write the critical comments you heard and your answer:

The critical remark was:
....
My answer is:
....
....

It can be very helpful to discuss this assignment with your therapist. Are your answers clear and are you able to defend yourself?

Showing Less Compliant Behaviour

Because of their fear of criticism from and rejection by others, eating disorder patients often want to conform to the expectations of others.

HELEN: 'I was always very much afraid that people might not accept me. I needed their approval and did my utmost to please others. In school I worked very hard to get good grades. Every night I studied very hard to get good results on my examinations. For my father it was so important that I had good grades, and I did not want to disappoint his expectations. But the price was very high, because I had to work very hard until late at night.'

JOYCE: 'The first thing my therapist told me was to learn to be clear in my mind about the reason why I do something: is that because I want to please others, or because I like to do it for myself? My therapist taught me to listen much better to myself instead of trying to comply with the expectations of others. At first I felt very egoistic, because I had learned that it was important to first give attention to others and that paying attention to yourself was negative and impolite. But I learned that other people can stand up for themselves, and you are also allowed to do that for yourself. That lesson was very important for me, and motivated me to change my ideas about myself. Now I can listen to myself much better and I no longer try to please others.'

In the treatment, the therapist can explain that listening to yourself does not mean that you are an egoist. It is a positive thing to take yourself seriously and there is no need to disregard your own feelings.

ANGELA: 'In the therapy I learned to listen much better to my own feelings, needs and desires. That was very difficult for me. I had never learned to do that and I often did not know what I really felt and thought. In the therapy I had to learn to take myself much more seriously and to listen to my own feelings and opinions. Now I feel much stronger and can stand up for myself much better.'

Assignment: Listening to one's own feelings and desires

It takes serious training to learn to become sensitive to what you feel and think without trying to please others. Make a list of your activities for today and describe why you are doing these things: is it because you want to please others, or do you like to do them for yourself? For this assignment, you need your notebook or diary. You can discuss your answers with your therapist.

1.   Activities which I do because I want to please others:

....

....

....

2. Activities which I like to do for myself:

....

....

....

When you do this assignment for the first time, it is possible that the list of activities you do in order to please others is much longer than the list of activities you do for yourself. The next time, try to make the list of things you want to do for yourself a little longer:

3. What might you do for yourself in the next week?

....

....

....

Having Less Perfectionism and Fear of Failure

Excessive perfectionism and fear of failure is very characteristic of eating disorder patients.

> ESTHER: 'Before my anorexia I always had high standards for myself. I wanted to do everything no less than perfectly and was only satisfied when I received the highest grades in school. In the treatment I learned that the reason for my perfectionism was that I was afraid to fail in the eyes of others. I was always afraid that I was not good enough, and in order to feel good about myself I needed to be better than others. I always had to prove myself. When I failed to get a high grade I felt very bad about myself. I was extremely afraid to fail. Even when I checked everything and studied for long hours I was still afraid to fail. I thought that failing in the eyes of others was the worst that could happen because my whole self-image would collapse. In the therapy I developed much more self-esteem and I learned to become less afraid of failure. If something does not go as I hoped I no longer think "I am failing" but I am able to think: "better luck next time".'

An important goal for psychotherapy is to reduce perfectionism and fear of failure.

> JEANNET: 'Even after my therapy I still want to do things as well as possible, but I am much less afraid to fail. Now I do things because I *like* to do them, not because I want to please others. I was always

extremely afraid to fail in the eyes of others. Now I can be glad when I receive a 70% grade. My self-image does not collapse when I do not get an 80% or 90% for my paper. I was always so afraid of failing and not being good enough. Now I can see that when you fail in one thing, you do not fail completely as a person. I have much more self-esteem and am less dependent on the approval of others. Failing is no disaster any more, but a challenge to learn, and to do it better the next time.'

AMY: 'Although I had very good results and often received positive feedback, I was always scared of failing during my first years in my job. I had the idea that once something went wrong my colleagues would discover my poor results. To prevent failure I worked as hard as I could and had very high standards. After my therapy I learned to value my qualities in a much more realistic way, without the fear to fail when I make a mistake.'

Questionnaire about improving psychological well-being

Which of the following aspects did you learn in this chapter?

You can answer 1 = no, 2 = a little, 3 = somewhat, 4 = yes, 5 = very high

1.	I have developed more self-esteem	1	2	3	4	5
2.	I have developed a better image of myself	1	2	3	4	5
3.	I no longer punish myself after food intake	1	2	3	4	5
4.	I have become less strict and perfectionist	1	2	3	4	5
5.	I have reduced my fear of failure	1	2	3	4	5
6.	I have developed a more realistic image of myself	1	2	3	4	5
7.	I have become less pleasing to others	1	2	3	4	5
8.	I have become less compliant to others	1	2	3	4	5
9.	I have become more assertive	1	2	3	4	5
10.	I stand up better for my own opinions	1	2	3	4	5

Other improvements of psychological well-being are:

11.	....	1	2	3	4	5
12.	....	1	2	3	4	5

If you have answered some questions with 1, 2 or 3, you can discuss your answers with your therapist, so that these areas can be taken into account and receive extra attention in the treatment. If you answered some questions with a 4 or 5, you have improved and try to continue in the same manner.

Summary

In this chapter, recovered patients described how they developed more self-esteem and self-respect. Psychotherapy helped them to correct their negative and critical images of themselves. They became more assertive and were less eager to comply with the expectations of others. They no longer try to please others and have become less dependent on the thoughts and opinions others may have about them. They were also able to reduce their perfectionism and fear of failure. Doing assignments and role-playing proved very helpful in achieving these goals. For patients, discovering what they want, think and feel and becoming more assertive takes much time and intensive training.

9

Expressing Emotions

Introduction

In the period before the development of an eating disorder, many patients find it difficult to express their emotions, especially negative feelings such as being disappointed, irritated, angry or furious (Beales & Dolton, 2000; Speranza, Loas, Wallier, & Corcos, 2007). They try to avoid and suppress these negative emotions and hide them from others. Extreme dieting helps them to suppress their negative sentiments (Jantz & Murray, 2002). However, when they stop dieting, the negative emotions return. To recover from an eating disorder, it is important to develop healthy strategies to cope with negative emotions. Patients have to learn that they may accept to have negative emotions and to express them, rather than avoiding and hiding them. Emotion regulation is a very important factor in combating an eating disorder (Elburg, 2007b; Zonnevijlle-Bender, van Goozen, Cohen-Kettenis, van Elberg, & van Engeland, 2004). Several treatment strategies are useful here, such as emotion focused therapy (Dolhanty & Greenberg, 2009), mindfulness (Baer, Fischer, & Huss, 2005; Kristeller et al., 2006), acceptance and commitment therapy (ACT) (Heffner & Eifert, 2004) and compassion-focused therapy (CFT) (Gilbert, 2010; Neff, 2003, 2011). In this chapter, recovered eating disorder patients describe how they learned to use healthier strategies to express their emotions.

Recovery from Eating Disorders: A Guide for Clinicians and Their Clients,
First Edition. Greta Noordenbos.
© 2013 John Wiley & Sons, Ltd. Published 2013 by John Wiley & Sons, Ltd.

No Longer Avoiding Negative Emotions

A first step in improving emotion regulation is to explore why patients have learned to avoid and suppress their negative emotions.

CATHY: 'My mother was often depressed, and when I sometimes felt disappointed or angry she started to cry, which made me feel guilty. I never learned to express my feelings of anger and disappointment. I always hid my real feelings from my mother because she already had so many problems and was so depressed. In the treatment I learned that it was normal to feel angry or disappointed and I did not have to feel guilty about these feelings. In order to learn to explore my negative feelings I first had to note them in my diary, and analyse why I was angry or disappointed, or felt grief and sorrow. This was a safe way to express myself, because nobody could read what I wrote down. After some weeks of training with noting down my negative feelings I had to learn to express my feelings to others both verbally and non-verbally. It was very important for me that my therapist reacted with appreciation when I expressed negative emotions. She accepted my feelings and understood why I felt disappointed or angry. This was very important for me, because I always thought that when I expressed my feelings of anger I would get very negative reactions from other people.'

JOCELYN: 'I was often afraid of becoming completely overwhelmed by negative emotions and tried to avoid them as much as possible. In the therapy I learned not to avoid or suppress my negative emotions, but to accept and explore them. I learned that it was not a bad thing to have negative emotions. There might be good reasons for becoming angry. My therapist used mindfulness training, which really helped me to become less afraid of being overwhelmed by negative feelings. I found that after a while my negative emotions became less extreme and finally disappeared, like a heavy thunder storm which blows over. Now I can regulate my negative emotions much better and do not need my eating behaviour to suppress them.'

Mindfulness seems to be a very useful strategy to help eating disorder patients to give careful attention to what they feel. This strategy helps them to become more sensitive to their physical sensations of being tired and cold, or hungry or satisfied (Kristeller et al., 2006). Mindfulness is also useful to learn to pay more attention to all kinds of psychological emotions and explore them instead of avoiding them.

After the first step of recognizing and exploring emotions, it is very important that patients learn to accept negative emotions as a part of their personality. For many eating disorder patients, it is difficult to accept that they have negative emotions.

JUDY: 'It took me a long time to accept that negative emotions are part of myself. I had always tried to avoid them and hide them from others. My parents did not allow me to express negative emotions such as anger, so that I learned that having these emotions is bad. I could not accept them as part of myself and felt I always had to be in a good mood. To others I only showed my positive emotions, even when I felt disappointed or angry. But that was not my real face, it was like a mask, but under that mask I often felt irritated and angry.'

HENRY: 'In the therapy I learned to express my negative emotions, even if not everybody might accept them. Exercises with role-playing were very helpful. After each exercise we discussed how we had reacted. At first I felt very bad when somebody became angry at me, and tried to become friendly again instead of expressing my own anger. But my therapist taught me that I was allowed to have negative feelings and be angry. This therapy was very helpful for me. After some months I realized that the inner tension and stress I often felt when I became angry or disappointed had become much lower and I dared to say outright why I was angry, without feeling guilty. I no longer feel the urge to binge when I feel angry. When I feel upset I first analyse my feelings in my diary and try to find out why I have become so annoyed. This helps me to reduce my tension and stress and the number of binges.'

Assignment: Feeling and expressing emotions

This assignment can help you analyse your negative feelings. Answer the following questions in your notebook or diary:

1. Which negative emotions do you feel (anger, disappointment, guilt, sadness, etc.)?
2. Which situation gave you those negative feelings?
3. Which strategies can you use to express your negative emotions?

As an example, refer to Jessica's answers:

1. I feel angry.
2. My sister criticized me about my appearance: she dislikes my hair and clothes.
3a. I can phone a friend and ask her to listen to me.
3b. If she does not answer, I can note my feelings in my diary.
3c. This evening, I will make it clear to my sister that I really felt bad about what she said to me.

And here are Hillary's answers:

1. I feel very disappointed.
2. My mother had promised to take me shopping and to buy new shoes for me. But this afternoon she told me that she wanted to stay at home,

because she felt very tired. I felt quite disappointed, but when I told her that she started to cry and said that I never understood how tired she was. Then I felt very guilty and tried to cheer her up.
3. I really felt disappointed and phoned a friend. She understood my feelings and suggested going shopping together on Saturday.

What are your answers?

1. I feel ....
2. That is because of ....
3. The following strategies might help me to feel better:
3a. ....
3b. ....
3c. ....

Reduction of Critical Thoughts and Inner Voices

Eating disorder patients often have very negative and critical thoughts about themselves. Although at first the dieting successes give them positive feelings, these feelings may sooner or later evaporate, while the negative and critical thoughts increase. These negative and critical thoughts are described by psychologists as *inner criticism* (Sterk & Swaen, 2006), *inner negativism* (Claude-Pierre, 1997) or *inner saboteur* (Kortink, 2008).

Noordenbos, Boesenach, Moerman, and Trommelen (2012) have shown that hearing negative inner thoughts or voices mostly starts at the beginning of the eating disorder, and the voice becomes more dominant at the later, serious stage of the disorder. The more strict and dominant the inner voice, the less patients are able to resist it. When their physical condition improves and they have more self-esteem, they learn to resist the messages from this inner voice. After recovering from their eating disorder, they are no longer dominated by their negative inner voice, which often disappears completely.

When patients are able to empower their self and their ego, their superego becomes less strict and they are better able to listen to their physical needs.

To develop any distance from their critical voice and superego, it is important for patients to develop a healthy way of thinking. Their feeling of *self* and self-respect has to become much stronger. They have to accept that they have physical needs and have to care for their body, which needs enough food, warmth, sleep and so on. Cognitive behavioural therapy (CBT) (Fairburn, Cooper, & Shafran, 2003) and CFT (Gilbert, 2010) can be very useful in reducing negative and critical thoughts. Suzan describes clearly how this therapeutic strategy helped her:

SUZAN: 'My therapist asked me to tell her what the inner voice said to me and to write that in my notebook. I told her that when I ate a piece of bread the inner voice criticised me: "You are eating too much, you can never resist food and you always fail. During the rest of the day you are not allowed to eat any more". Together we analysed whether the message of that negative voice was right and fair. My therapist also helped me to give feedback to my inner voice. For example: "Why is one piece of bread too much for a girl of 18 years old? It is necessary to nourish your body, and one piece of bread is not enough. You say that I always fail. But that is not true, because I successfully did my homework this morning, and I was able to go to school just in time". Together with my therapist I analysed why the inner voice was not right, and then I had to learn to give my reaction and write that answer in my notebook. For example: "Every human body needs enough food. Without enough food you cannot live. I am a human person and I need enough food to nourish my body. To eat one piece of bread during lunch is not too much for an 18-year-old girl". Each week I became better at developing arguments against the critical voice in my head. I became much stronger and felt less overwhelmed by the disapproving voice. After a while the messages from the voice became less frequent and less dominant, and at the end of the therapy the voice had nearly vanished. I was much better able to find arguments against my inner critic, and was able to resist its messages. I learned to perceive the negative voice as thoughts in my own head which can come and go. I no longer have to obey all the orders of that critical voice.'

At the first stage of the treatment, most eating disorder patients are not able to resist their negative thoughts or inner voices and need the help of a therapist. With the help of their therapist, they can analyse the negative and unfair commands of their inner critical voice and can find arguments to defend themselves against this inner critic. The more the patients learn to defend themselves by healthy arguments, the less they need the support of their therapist. Finally, they are able to cope with their inner critical voices.

BIANCA: 'In the first period my therapist helped me to answer the extreme and unfair criticism from my inner voice. After some time my therapist asked me to develop my own answers and to tell them to her. She taught me to make my answers clearer and louder. After some time I felt much stronger and more empowered against that critical inner voice. Finally I was even able to get angry at the voice, and to stop it or send it away. I said, for example "There you are again: I hate your negative messages and you are always criticising me. You never say positive things to me. I will not listen to you any more." Every time I hear that negative voice I am able to find clear arguments against doing what the voice commands. I feel much stronger and more empowered. In the therapy I also learned to say positive things to myself and even to give myself a compliment: For example: "well done, I have earned a compliment". Why should I always be kind to others and not to myself?'

FARIDAH: 'I am so glad that my therapist taught me how to analyse the negative messages from my inner voice, and to defend myself against all the criticism. I will never again be dominated by that negative voice which destroyed all pleasure in my life.'

SIMONE: 'Fortunately my therapist supported me against all the negative commands in my head. She always believed in the healthy part of my personality, even when that was very small. Later on my sister became a great support. She realised that she also had many negative thoughts about herself. Then we started to help each other to develop more positive thoughts about ourselves. My sister helped me to look at my positive sides and I was able to help my sister to see hers. That was very helpful.'

Assignment: Defence against inner critical thoughts

Most eating disorder patients feel overwhelmed and dominated by their negative thoughts and inner voices. They often are unable to resist the commands of these thoughts or voices. However, they do have a choice. They do not need to obey the voice's negative commands. They can empower their positive and healthy side, even though it might have become very weak. So it is important to empower their healthy thoughts and to develop a positive voice in their head. The following assignments can be very helpful in defending yourself against your inner negative thoughts and voices.

Write down the content of your negative thoughts or voices on the left-hand side of your diary or notebook. This helps create some distance between you and these thoughts or voices. Describing them enables you to analyse their content and to talk about them with your therapist. You do not have to believe what the negative thoughts and voices tell you; you can develop alternative thoughts which are more positive and healthy for you and can comfort you. On the right-hand side of the page, write your reaction to the negative thoughts or voices.

This is what Sophy wrote in her notebook: 'When I ate even one slice of bread my negative inner voice said to me: You eat too much, you will never become slim. Today you are not allowed to eat anything else.'

My answer is: 'Why am I not allowed to eat any more today? What you want is unfair and not good for my health. I just ate one piece of bread. That is not too much. I need more food to nourish my body. Your commands are not positive and beneficial for me. I no longer want to obey your negative and punishing orders. You make me very unhappy and always give me the feeling I have failed. So I no longer want to listen to you and to do what you tell me. My healthy side says I should eat enough and at least three regular meals. I will have dinner this evening and I am allowed to eat some pasta, fish and vegetables.'

Now you can write down your own negative thoughts, followed by your positive thoughts:

My negative thoughts are: My reaction is:
....
....
....
....
....

In order to reduce the impact of your inner negative thoughts and voices, and to empower your positive and caring thoughts and voices, you have to repeat this assignment frequently. Every time you have negative thoughts and voices in your head, write them in your notebook and analyse their content. What do they say? Are they right and fair? What might be your positive answer?

It can be very helpful to discuss your answers with your therapist and to train yourself until your negative thoughts and voices no longer dominate your life. By doing this assignment frequently, you will empower your healthy side and learn to think in a more positive way about yourself.

Assignment: Developing ideal compassion image and feelings

For some people, it is very difficult to think in a positive and caring way about themselves. The following assignment, developed in CFT, can be very helpful (Gilbert, 2010, p. 190).

First step: Create your ideal compassion image.
  A compassion image is warm, accepting and deeply committed to you.
  You can choose any image that gives you these feelings. This might be a real person, but also a fairytale character, a spiritual person, the sun, an animal or a flower.

Answering the following questions can help you create your compassion image:

What would you like your ideal caring compassion image to be?

1. To look like?..
2. To sound like?..
3. To feel like?..
4. How should it relate to you?...
5. How would you relate to your ideal caring-compassion image?............

What do you really want from feeling compassion from other people? Try to be clear what you really want: protection, understanding, to be known, to feel valued or cared for?

Your ideal caring-compassion image wants to help you and is deeply committed to you and your longings and desires. This compassion image really wants to relieve your suffering.

When you start to think in a positive way about yourself, you first make contact with your ideal caring-compassion image in order to feel free, safe and valued.

It is desirable that you create these feelings within you so that you gradually learn to focus on compassion for yourself rather than on self-criticism. Practicing self-compassion is an important strategy to learn to accept yourself as you really are.

Recognizing and Expressing Emotions

For most eating disorder patients, it is difficult to recognize and express their emotions. Although they are often very sensitive to the emotions of others, they have not learned to be sensitive to their own feelings. They often use their eating disorder as a strategy to avoid and suppress their own feelings and emotions.

ANNABEL: 'I remember that I really did not know what my own feelings were. I always directed my attention to the feelings and thoughts of my mother, who was often depressed. I tried to hide my negative emotions from my mother, because she already had so many problems. I completely lost contact with my own feelings and emotions. When I started dieting and my weight decreased I experienced emotions less and less, and after some time I felt quite numb and did not feel my emotions at all any more. In the treatment I had to learn to explore my feelings and emotions, instead of avoiding and suppressing them. When I started the treatment my therapist often asked how I felt. I could only say that I felt sad and grey. In the treatment I had to eat more and to gain weight, which frightened me. I had very strong feelings of fear and wanted to suppress them by dieting and losing weight. However, my therapist asked me not to avoid and suppress my fears, but to accept that I had these feelings and express them. When I did that I realized that after a while my feelings of panic became less.'

BOB: 'During the first part of the treatment my emotions were very negative and overwhelming, but the therapist taught me that when I became more sensitive to my feelings and wrote down what I felt, these emotions would become less threatening and intense. Slowly I learned to differentiate between various kinds of emotions. For me it was very important to learn that it is not bad to have negative emotions. It was new to me to accept that I was allowed to be angry, disappointed or sad. I no longer avoid and suppress these feelings but have learned to accept and express them.'

CAROLA: 'When I was young it was not done in my family to express negative emotions, or to show yourself disappointed or angry. I developed the idea that having negative emotions was not accepted by my parents and I tried to hide them from others. In the treatment, however, I learned that it is not wrong or bad to have negative emotions or to feel angry. There might be good reasons to be disappointed or annoyed. My therapist encouraged me to express these emotions instead of hiding and avoiding them. She tried to understand why I had these negative feelings, and together we explored why I felt bad, guilty or angry. She accepted me with all my emotions and I did not have to hide them from her, on the contrary. For the first time in my life I could tell somebody how bad I felt and how angry I was about all the carping I got from my mother. I felt sad for not being accepted by my mother, sad that she never paid any attention to my emotions. In the therapy I felt safe to explore and express my negative feelings, and I felt accepted together with all my emotions, even when they were negative. That was a very new experience for me and helped me to reduce my binges. I no longer needed a binge in order to suppress my negative emotions.'

Anorectic and bulimic patients find it difficult to get in touch with their emotions, to differentiate between them and to describe them. They can have alexithymia, which means that they are not able to read and describe their emotions adequately (Jimerson, Wolfe, Franko, Covino, & Sifneos, 1994). Bulimic patients often have a general feeling of distress before a binge without being able to describe their emotions.

In the treatment, it is important that the therapist be able to explore and accept patients' negative emotions and understand why they have these feelings. Recent therapies aimed at exploring and accepting emotions are *mindfulness* (Baer, Fischer, & Huss, 2005; Kristeller et al., 2006) and ACT (Hayes, Strosahl, & Wilson, 1999; Heffner & Eifert, 2004).

AFFY: 'In the therapy I learned that I used my binges as a strategy to suppress my "forbidden" negative emotions. The more I learned to accept and to explore my emotions, and the more I learned to analyse why I felt that way, the less I felt the urge to binge.'

MARY: 'During the Cognitive Behavioural Treatment I learned much about my cognitions but I could not *feel* my emotions. To be able to recover from my eating disorder I had to get in touch with my emotions. In the Acceptance and Commitment therapy I learned no longer to avoid my emotions, but to accept them as part of myself. The more I learned to accept that I was allowed to have negative emotions, the less I needed my eating disorder to suppress them.'

DAN: 'In the therapy I learned to eat three regular meals during the day so that the physical need to have a binge became much less. But I also learned to reduce my psychological tension and stress by listening more sensitively to my emotions. I was asked to analyse why I had these negative emotions, and to note them in my diary. After some time I became much better at defending myself when a colleague made critical comments to my face. When I have negative experiences, such as a printer that won't work, I can now remain more relaxed. When it is really necessary to print something I go to another department in my office and ask to use their printer. When I come home I feel less stress. I often start with having a walk, which makes me more relaxed. This is very helpful to reduce my binges.'

JEANNET: 'Before my eating disorder I often did not know what I felt and I was not able to express my emotions. I was always afraid that people would not like me any more when I expressed my negative feelings. For that reason I always kept up appearances by saying that I liked something, while deep down inside me I did not like it. I always said yes and tried to please others, even when I felt quite unhappy. It was not only other people that I had to keep up appearances for, but also myself, because having negative emotions did not fit the image I had of myself. In the treatment I learned that everybody has negative feelings, and that it is not at all bad to have them.'

SUZY: 'In the treatment I learned that it is important to listen to your emotions, and not to avoid or to suppress them. I have learned to be honest with myself and to express my real emotions instead of adapting to the expectations of others. When I feel that something is not right for me I try to analyse what kind of feelings I have: fear, anger or disappointment? I have become much better at expressing my emotions without being afraid of hurting others, or being criticized by them.'

Dare to Express Different Opinions

Eating disorder patients often find it very difficult to disagree or come into conflict with somebody because they are afraid to be rejected by others. Therefore, they adjust their opinions to those of others and hide their own views. However, by doing this often, they no longer know what they really think themselves. An important goal for treatment is for patients to explore and express their real feelings and opinions and to reduce their fear of being criticized or rejected when they express their own thoughts and opinions. They have to learn that being criticized by others does not mean that they are no longer accepted.

NATASCHA: 'I was always afraid of having a conflict, because I thought that other people would then not like me any more. For that reason I hid my real opinions from others. In the treatment I learned that I can have different opinions, and express them without being rejected as a person. People can disagree and still respect each other. I had to learn to have more respect for my own opinion. In the treatment I had to practise expressing my own thoughts and opinions in role plays. In the first stage of the therapy it was very difficult for me to stand up for my opinion, and I often gave in to the views of others. But the therapist stimulated me to express my own arguments instead of agreeing with others. I had to learn to convince others of my opinion. That was quite difficult for me, because I always had been very compliant and eager to please. Now I am very glad that I dare to express my own opinions and arguments. I do not feel bad or rejected any more when others think differently.'

THALIA: 'Before my eating disorder I was always very scared of having a conflict with somebody and I tried very hard to prevent that. To me, having a conflict meant that others criticize you, become angry at you and no longer accept you. I found that very threatening. In the therapy I learned to express my own opinions and arguments and I am no longer afraid when other people have different opinions. I have learned that you can have different opinions or even a conflict and still be seen as a respectable person.'

In the treatment, patients have to learn that it is normal for people to have different opinions and sometimes have a conflict. Having a conflict does not mean that other people reject you as a person. A conflict can be discussed, and sometimes you will end up concluding that you disagree. Many conflicts can be solved without serious problems.

CHRISTINE: 'It was an eye-opener for me to realise that I can have my own opinions and not be criticized because of them. I no longer give in to others and I have become much more convinced of my own opinions. I no longer try to comply with the opinions of others or do my best to please them.'

JOCELYNE: 'I will never become a person who likes conflicts, but when I have a disagreement with somebody I no longer try to comply and to please. I first analyse what the problem is about and why we disagree. I take some time to get clear what my arguments and feelings are, because I have never learned to take my own opinions seriously and to stand up for myself. I also learned that when you often have serious conflicts it might be better to finish a relationship. When I found I had many conflicts with my former boyfriend I had the courage to finish my relationship with him without feeling guilty or bad about it. We were just too different and it was better to go our separate ways.'

Assignment: Coping with different opinions and conflicts

On the left-hand side of your diary or notebook, write the reason for a conflict, and on the right-hand side, try to analyse the content of the conflict and give your own arguments.

Here is an assignment that was completed by Fenny:

Conflict: My boyfriend complained that I never wanted to go to a film with him. *Argument*: It is not true that I never want to go to a film, but I do not like the film he chose.

Several months ago we saw a very nice film. But that was two months ago, and that might be the reason that he was angry and disappointed when I did not join him.
Solution: I will phone him, explain my opinion and ask him if we could try to find another film, which we both like.

Now describe in your notebook a conflict you have had.
....

What are your arguments?
....

Which suggestions can you find for a solution?
....

Discuss your answers with your therapist. What can you learn from having a conflict?

No Longer Feeling Depressed

An important aim in extreme dieting is to feel less sad and depressed and more upbeat. Although the first effect of dieting is a general improvement in mood, these positive feelings sooner or later fade away. After some time, patients feel even more sad and depressed. Anorectic patients who have a very low weight often feel numb and do not feel their emotions any more; their feelings have been suppressed by starvation. However, when they eat more and their weight increases, they again feel all the negative emotions they tried to avoid. The first reaction is often to suppress these negative feelings again by extreme dieting. Much psychological support is needed at this stage to prevent relapse.

CHRISTINE: 'At the most critical stage of my anorexia nervosa my feelings and emotions were completely suppressed and I felt very numb. When my weight increased I felt pessimistic and depressed. In order to avoid these negative emotions I started extreme dieting again, and then I really got into a deep pit. Finally I had to admit that dieting was not the solution to my negative emotions. I decided to go to a clinic for eating disorders where I learned to eat more. Slowly my depression cleared up and I was able to think and feel again. For the first time in a long time I felt a little more relaxed and I could laugh again. That motivated me to continue my treatment.'

Psycho-education about the relationship between food and emotions is a very useful part of the treatment. Patients have to learn that lack of food, starvation, binges and vomiting have severe consequences not only for their weight but also for their mood (Jantz & Mc Murray, 2002).

CHRISTA: 'Because of my extreme diet I became severely depressed, and the less I ate the more depressed I felt. I constantly thought that I had to lose more weight and continue my diet in order to feel better. From my therapist I learned that not only my body, but also my brains need nutrients in order to feel less depressed. She told me that some important nutrients that make you feel less depressed can be found in chocolate, bananas, fatty fish and fish oil. But I always thought that I would become obese if I took these nutrients so they had become "forbidden food" for me. My therapist explained that one of the reasons I felt so sad and depressed was that I lacked basic nutrients in my body and brains. She told me about the function of serotonin, a neurotransmitter which is very important for your mood. In the treatment I learned that my ideas about food were quite wrong, and even harmful for my body and mind. She taught me that if I ate more I would become less depressed and feel much better. This information made me more motivated to eat a little more and to gain weight. I was very glad that the therapist allowed me to take small steps, but she was very strict: each step had to be followed by a next step. After several weeks I had gradually come to feel a little better, and that motivated me to continue to increase my food intake and weight. I had more energy for other things and felt more relaxed. I realised that enough food is important not only for my body, but also for my mood.'

Psycho-education and cognitive behaviour therapy are very important strategies to correct disturbed cognitions about food and weight. In order to feel the first positive results, patients have to eat sufficient amounts of food very regularly during several weeks. However, when eating disorder patients are very depressed, they need more than healthy food to recover. For severely depressed patients, antidepressants might be helpful (Nice Guidelines for Eating Disorders, 2004).

ROSALY: 'When my depression did not clear up my psychiatrist prescribed antidepressants. After a few weeks I started to feel a little better. Not only did my depressive feelings become less, but my feelings of fear also diminished. That was very important for me because I was extremely anxious and depressed. At the first stage of my treatment I needed these antidepressants in order to reduce my extreme depression and anxiety. Later on I experienced that eating regular meals containing sufficient healthy nutrients was the best "medication" against my negative emotions.'

Questionnaire about improving emotion regulation

The following questions are about improving emotion regulation.

You can answer 1 = no, 2 = a little, 3 = somewhat, 4 = yes, 5 = very much

1.	I no longer suppress negative emotions	1	2	3	4	5
2.	I am less afraid to have negative emotions	1	2	3	4	5
4.	I no longer avoid my emotions	1	2	3	4	5
5.	I have learned to listen better to my emotions	1	2	3	4	5
6.	I have learned to express negative emotions	1	2	3	4	5
7.	I have learned to express positive emotions	1	2	3	4	5
8.	I can cope better with feelings of stress	1	2	3	4	5
9.	I feel less depressed	1	2	3	4	5

Other improvements of coping better with my emotions: 1   2   3   4   5

10.	....	1	2	3	4	5
11.	....	1	2	3	4	5
12.	....	1	2	3	4	5

If you have answered some questions with 1, 2 or 3, you can discuss your answers with your therapist, so that these areas can be taken into account and receive extra attention in the treatment. If you answered some questions with a 4 or 5, you have improved and try to continue in the same manner.

Summary

This chapter was about coping with emotions, especially negative emotions, which often play an important role in the development and continuation of eating disorders. The eating disorder often functions as a strategy to avoid and suppress negative emotions. Some eating disorder patients have lost all contact with their own feelings, opinions and desires. Therefore, it is important that they learn to recognize their negative emotions and to express them, instead of avoiding and suppressing them. In this chapter, recovered patients described how important it was for them to become more sensitive to their own feelings and emotions. They learned that it is not necessarily a bad thing to have negative emotions or to be angry. They learned to accept these feelings and to analyse why they had these negative emotions, and which alternative strategies they could use to regulate them. They also learned to express their own opinions and to become more assertive. All these experiences helped them to become less depressed and anxious. Instead of regulating their negative emotions by extreme dieting or by binging and purging, they developed better coping strategies for their negative emotions.

10

Improving Social Relations

Introduction

As a consequence of eating disorders, patients become more and more isolated. They withdraw from social activities because they want to hide their eating problems from others. Anorectic patients often start to skip parties and dinners because they fear they have to eat there. Bulimic patients are afraid that they cannot keep control over their food intake and will not be able to vomit or to use laxatives.

When the physical consequences of their eating disorder become serious, patients often lack the energy to meet other people. At the most critical stage, they are no longer able to go to school or work. Their social world becomes very small and only a few contacts are left. Parents, siblings and a few friends are the only persons who try to keep in touch. However, it is difficult for them to remain in contact with the patient at the most severe stage of the eating disorder, because they become depressed and numb.

To recover from an eating disorder, it is not only physical and psychological improvement that is important but also improving social relations (Rorty, Yager, Buckwalter, & Rossotto, 1999). Patients have to learn to make contact with peers and to make friends. In order to be able to make contact with others, they need to feel physically fit and develop more self-esteem and better social coping strategies. They have to become less eager to please and more assertive. For developing better contacts, social support is very relevant. Self-help groups or group therapy can be a first step towards making more contact with other people. In the therapy, patients have to learn to take initiatives and to become less afraid of revealing their personal

Recovery from Eating Disorders: A Guide for Clinicians and Their Clients,
First Edition. Greta Noordenbos.
© 2013 John Wiley & Sons, Ltd. Published 2013 by John Wiley & Sons, Ltd.

thoughts and emotions. In this chapter, recovered eating disorder patients describe how they improved their social relations and how they were able to continue their education and career.

Learning to Trust other People

At the most critical stage of their eating disorder, most patients have strong feelings of distrust towards others, because they fear that they will force them to change their eating habits. Even in their diary, they do not dare to write honestly about what they really think and feel, because they are afraid that other people might read what they have written.

> LINDA: 'For a long time my diary was the only place where I could write about what really worried me, and what I ate and how I felt about that. But in the long run I no longer dared to write what I really thought or did, because my mother might find my diary. So I just wrote about ordinary things, or even lied about what was really going on in my mind.'

For therapists, parents and friends, it is often very difficult to trust the patient, and the patient often does not yet dare to trust them. An important step is to restore the feeling of trust.

> MARISKA: 'At some moment there was nobody who trusted me any longer. And to be honest I could not be trusted concerning my food intake and weight. I often was dishonest about what I ate. But when I finally felt that I had sunk into a deep pit and nobody could help me any more, I met a therapist who told me that she trusted me and believed that I could recover. That was very important for me. The therapist trusted me! She convinced me that I was valuable person and she accepted me, even with my eating disorder and all my problems. She told me that the most important goal was to become a bit happier and to learn to enjoy life again. And she said that she believed I was able to improve, even if at that moment it was so difficult for me to believe that. She constantly told me that I was a valuable person and believed that I could recover. Knowing that my therapist trusted me was so important for me that I slowly learned to trust her and dared to tell her about all the problems I had.'

It is remarkable that many eating disorders patients said that for them it was very important that other people believed that they were able to recover long before even they could believe it themselves. This trust from others, whether parents, a therapist or a friend, was crucial to their process of recovery. Many patients, however, found that others no longer trusted them and did not believe they might overcome their disorder.

WENDELA: 'When you have an eating disorder many therapists expect you to trust them and believe in their treatment. But for me it was relevant that my therapist trusted me. I was so happy to find a therapist who believed in me as a valuable person, even when I was not always honest about my food and weight. The therapist told me that it was the anorexia which made me dishonest. She made a difference between my "real self", which could be trusted, and the anorexia, which was dishonest. She told me that she wanted to make contact with my real self, even if it was very weak. It was important to empower my real self, and together we would fight against the anorexia that forced me to continue my eating disorder. My therapist helped me to make my real self much stronger, and the anorectic voice in me became weaker and weaker.'

Treatment of anorexia patients is very difficult because their *anorectic voice* is often very strong and dominates their life. For the therapist, it is important to focus on the patient's healthy side and to reduce the negative voice of the eating disorder. To empower this healthy side, it is crucial to listen to the patients' feelings and emotions. This was a basic condition for Fanny's recovery process:

FANNY: 'For me it was so important that somebody could accept me how I was, without condemning me, even when I was very anorectic. My therapist was able to see my strong and healthy points without forgetting my weak points. She always supported me in spite of all my difficulties and setbacks. The therapist strongly believed in my ability to overcome my anorexia.'

Building a stable relationship with a therapist is an essential condition for recovery. A stable relationship requires continuation of the contact with a specific therapist for quite a long time. For patients, it can be difficult to meet different therapists frequently and to establish a new relationship every time. Continuity of the therapeutic relationship is important for a safe and positive attachment without the fear of losing that contact or being rejected by the therapist. A stable, positive and supporting relationship is a basic condition for developing new social contacts and to break through patients' isolation.

Participating in Social Activities

It is often difficult for eating disorder patients to initiate contacts because they are afraid of negative reactions from others. The first contacts often have to be initiated by others. Group therapy and self-help groups can be very supportive of participation in social activities, which are often initiated by the therapist. For patients, these contacts with fellow sufferers are often the first step towards getting out of their isolation.

> JANE: 'At the most critical stage of my anorexia I had become very isolated. When I was admitted to a clinic for eating disorders I had to participate in different group activities. At first it was very difficult for me to make contact with other patients. It was very confrontational to see that other girls were more emaciated than I was. But I also felt reassured that I was not the only person who was obsessed by food and weight. In the clinic I came into contact with a few other anorectic girls and learned that they had the same fears, thoughts and feelings. I no longer felt so lonely with my problems. After some time I felt less alone in this clinic, where they understood me much better than my parents and brothers did. At home they did not understand why I did not eat more and they were angry with me, so that I tried to avoid contact with them as much as possible.'

It is important for eating disorder patients to become involved in social activities.

> KAREN: 'I was always very shy and in the worst period of my eating disorders I had become completely isolated and felt very lonely. When I came to the clinic the therapist and other patients asked me questions that I was required to answer. I learned to develop more initiatives in social contacts. I also had to tell them more about myself, which was very threatening for me. At first I only told people about general experiences and activities, but later on I dared to say more about my personal experiences and emotions. In the months I stayed in the clinic I developed very good contacts with some girls and made some real friends. We still discuss many problems about food and weight and can always stimulate each other to find solutions. We are not afraid to tell each other about our weak points and risks of relapse, and we help each other to think and behave in a more positive way.'

Not everybody needs group therapy in a clinic for eating disorders to learn to make better contact. Vicky said that for her it was helpful that she went to a self-help group were she dared to talk about her eating disorder:

> VICKY: 'In that self-help group I was not afraid to say that I had an eating disorder. It was no longer necessary to hide my disorder from them and I felt less lonely with my problems. When they knew about my eating disorder I no longer had to try so hard to act as if I had no problems with food and weight. The tension became less and I felt much more relaxed.'

It is important for eating disorder patients to feel accepted by others even when they have many problems. They need to feel *safe* to talk about their problems and not forced to change their eating habits and weight. The feeling of being accepted even with their eating problems was an important condition to speak about their problems more openly.

JOAN: 'People often say that eating disorder patients lie and cannot be trusted. I felt very angry about that prejudice, because the reason I did not tell the truth was that I was so afraid that people might force me to eat. I also felt ashamed when others discovered that I had an eating disorder. When some of my friends read more about bulimia and understood that I felt so afraid and ashamed to talk about my binging and purging behaviour, they understood much better why I had never told them about my eating problems. When they understood my fear and yet did not reject me or became angry at me, I felt much more relaxed and became more honest about my eating behaviour. My friends were very important for me in the process of recovery.'

ANGELA: 'When my friends knew I had an eating disorder I was able to visit them without being pushed to eat. If I said that I did not like to come to a party, they told me that it was OK if I did not eat anything, or only those things I wanted to eat. They told me that they wanted to see me as a person rather than an eating disorder patient. We no longer talked about my food intake and weight: these topics I discussed with my therapist. For me it was very important to have a few friends with whom I could talk about other things which are relevant for me. My friends helped me to become less isolated. They assured me that they accepted me as a valuable person, even if I had an eating disorder.'

Education and Career

During the process of recovery, it is important to develop several social activities. For young patients, their school education is just as relevant as having contacts with peers. For Daniella, however, it was very difficult to return to school:

DANIELLA: 'In the most critical period of my eating disorder I was no longer able to go to school, but at home I had contact only with my parents. I realised that it was important go to school again and continue my education. When I had recovered quite well in the clinic for eating disorders I discussed with my therapist how to continue my education, but I did not want to go back to my former school. I had had many negative experiences there, with classmates first nicknaming me as "fatty" and later "skinny". I really hated that school. So we decided to look for another school where I could make a new start, and where they would not know me as ano-rexia patient. We found another school in which not only my intellectual capacities but also my creative talents could be developed. In the clinic I had discovered that I like to work with colours and textiles. So I chose a school that offered courses about fashion. That was a very good decision. Nobody knew that I had been in a clinic for eating disorders, I made some friends and after some time I dared to tell them about my history of anorexia. Now I have made several friends in that school and really feel accepted.'

For adult patients, it is important to have a job or to do voluntary work. Nicole always liked her job but could not continue when she had a severe eating disorder:

NICOLE: 'After leaving the clinic it was very important for me to return to my job. But that was quite confrontational, because the last period at work had been extremely difficult. During the day I did not allow myself to eat, but when I came home I felt extremely tired and stressed and had a huge binge, followed by purging and taking laxatives. Then I was completely exhausted and soon fell asleep on my couch. During the night, however, I was often awake for hours. I felt hungry so that I finally went to the kitchen just to get some bread. Then, when I started to eat some bread I lost control and had a second binge during the night. I fell asleep around 4 am. When I heard my alarm clock at 7.30 I was extremely tired and often had a severe headache so that I was unable to go to work. But when I stayed at home my binges and purges became even more frequent. Finally I was no longer able to work and was admitted to a clinic for eating disorders. It was not easy to recover, but I really wanted to get better. After six months I was able to return to work. I was very glad that my colleagues welcomed me. At first I only worked in the mornings, but after some weeks I started to work whole days. Now I am one year further on, and I go to my office every day and feel so much better. I am really proud of myself for having succeeded in winning that terrible struggle against my bulimia.'

For patients, reintegration in the labour market is important not only to increase social contacts but also to develop more self-esteem and to improve their financial position.

HILDE: 'I was so glad that I found a new job. During my bulimia I felt worthless and isolated, and I had serious debts because of all the binges and laxatives. I guess that during my bulimia my debts were very high. For many years I was unable to have a holiday. Together with a financial specialist I made a plan to repay my debts within two years. Now I can save money, and I have planned a holiday with my friend. It feels great that I can make this tour and can pay for it myself. I am really happy that I am no longer a prisoner of my bulimia.'

Having a job or doing voluntary work is important for patients for developing their talents.

GRACE: 'My job is very important for me, because it gives me the possibility to develop my skills. In my job I can contribute to society, which is very satisfying.'

It is not always easy to find a job after recovery from an eating disorder. Doing voluntary work can be a good alternative and also yields valuable social contacts.

MIRJAM: 'After my treatment I started to do some voluntary work for the Foundation for Eating Disorders. I had very good experiences with my treatment and wanted to share that experience with patients who are still looking for treatment. Now I am a guide for a self-help group. I feel that others can learn from my positive experiences while recovering from my bulimia nervosa. I am not only involved in activities related to eating disorders, but am also following a course about communication. In the weekend I have my hobbies, painting and singing in a choir. I am involved in many social activities and made new friends so I no longer feel isolated.'

After recovery from their eating disorder, some patients discovered that the course of education they followed, or the job they had, was not really what they wanted, and they decided to change their education or job. The story of Lucy is a clear illustration:

LUCY: 'Before my eating disorder my father had advised me to have a finance job in a big business company. Although I earned a good salary I was not very happy with that job. I did what others expected me to do, but that was not what I really wanted. In the therapy it became clear that I had always been eager to comply with the expectations of others, such as my father and my colleagues. It took some time before I discovered what I really liked. Finally I dared to take a huge step and found another job with more social contacts. Although my income is less, I feel happier and do my job with much more pleasure. I feel so much richer compared with my former job, which brought only superficial glamour but was emotionally not very satisfying. At first my father did not agree with my decision, but now he supports my choice because he sees that I feel so much better.'

Intimate Relations

Many recovered patients stated that in the period before their eating disorder their contacts with others were quite superficial, because they did not feel secure enough to talk about their deeper emotions and opinions. In the therapy, their self-esteem grows, and they learn to have the courage to talk about their inner thoughts and emotions. This is an important condition for developing more intimate contacts.

> RACHEL: 'It took a long time before I was able to tell my friends about my deeper emotions and worries. Before my eating disorder we talked about this and that. At some moment one of my friends became angry and said to me: "I often tell you about myself, but you never say anything about what you really think or feel. I have the feeling you are hiding lots of things from me". I was distressed and disappointed about this confrontation, but she was right. And then I told her for the first time how insecure I often felt about myself, and that I was always afraid others might not accept me. To my delight she reacted in an emphatic way and said that she would support me if I wanted to tell her more about myself. So each time we meet we try to tell each other what is really important in our lives. I am glad that I can really trust her.'

It is difficult for eating disorder patients to become more open about their thoughts and emotions. It is even more difficult for them to develop physical intimacy, because they also feel insecure about their body and are very afraid of being criticized. For Bonny, this negative evaluation of her body was an obstacle to developing positive feelings about a sexual relationship.

> BONNY: 'In the clinic for eating disorders we received psycho-sexual education in a group, and I learned much about the function of the female body. For me it was very important to hear that many girls found it difficult to develop breasts and to have periods. We learned to talk about our own experiences and how to develop a more positive body attitude. That helped me to indeed view my body in a more positive light.'

Judith had a very negative attitude towards sexual contacts. For her it was important to receive information about the function of the female body and to talk about sexual experiences.

> JUDITH: 'In the therapy I learned that erotic contacts can be pleasant. That was new for me because I had had many negative experiences with boys. We learned to talk about our own erotic ideas and feelings.

I like nice clothes and once I went with a group of anorectic girls to a lingerie shop to buy a bra we liked. I found a very beautiful small bra, but even that was too big for me. For the first time I wanted to have breasts, because then I could wear that lovely bra, and when it finally fit me I felt very feminine. Now I'm looking forward to finding a nice bikini for my summer holidays.'

In the treatment, it is important to learn to develop more positive feelings about having a female body.

SUZY: 'For me it was very important to learn that I could express all my feelings about my body. My attitude towards sexuality changed in a positive way. Before my eating disorder I always had very negative feelings about sexuality because I was always afraid that I might lose control over my body and become an object in the eyes of men.'

Negative sexual experiences can play an important role in the development of an eating disorder.

WENDY: 'Several of the boys at school had tried to have sex with me, saying that it was very normal to have sex. They mentioned some popular girls in school who already had regular sexual contacts with boys. I felt very confused and negative about myself when they told me that I was old-fashioned. But when I finally had sex with one of these boys it was a very disappointing experience. Although he was very kind to me before, he did not show any affection afterwards and just went off. After that first "quickie" I felt very bad about myself and my body. I never dared to talk about my negative emotions. Although it was no rape because I had agreed, it felt as if I only had been "used for sex". Or was it because he did not like my body? Did he leave me because I was not as attractive as the other girls in my class? I felt very bad about my body and decided to go on a diet. In the therapy I learned that I should always listen to my own feelings and never do something I did not like, and that boys who really like you respect your choices. My self-esteem increased and I felt much stronger. Now I am no longer impressed by the popular boys and girls in my class. They are not my types. I have much more self-esteem and I've learned to be more proud of my body.'

Henriette, too, has changed her negative attitude towards sexuality and has developed a much more positive view of herself, her body and sexual contacts.

HENRIETTE: 'When I had an eating disorder I hated physical contact. I found it disgusting. But when I had recovered quite well I fell in love with a very nice boy from my school. That was the first time I liked to touch him, and to be touched by him. At first all that was very new for me and I still felt insecure about my body. But we were really in love with each other and that was quite different from just having sex for one night. I told him about my anorexia nervosa, and he was very kind and caring to me. My first sexual experience was with all lights out. It was just this physical experience of being touched all over my body. I knew that he could not see my body and that helped a lot. Slowly I learned to enjoy having physical contact with him and later on I was no longer afraid that he saw my naked body. Now I feel very safe with him.'

Pregnancy and Children

For women with an eating disorder, especially anorectic women, pregnancy is often an ambivalent experience, even when they really want children. For general practitioners and therapists, it is important to explore patients' attitude towards becoming pregnant and their growing belly. When eating disorder patients are pregnant, they often feel the need to control their weight and are very scared of becoming overweight. For Emma, it was a real struggle between wanting a baby and keeping her weight under control:

> EMMA: 'When I finally got pregnant I was in two minds about my growing belly. I really wanted to have a baby but I was also frightened to see my belly swell. I had the feeling I was losing control over my body. I struggled with my positive feelings about becoming a mother and my negative feelings about my weight increase. Of course I knew that dieting was very bad for the baby, because it might not grow enough and even run an increased risk of being born too early. I discussed all these ambivalent feelings with my therapist. It was very helpful for me to be able to distinguish between my own body and the baby's. I learned that it was not only my body which was growing, but also, and much more, the baby growing inside me. After the baby had been born my body would become quite normal again after a few months. That reassured me very much, so that I was finally able to resist my urge to diet.'

It is not only the period of pregnancy that can be difficult for women who have an eating disorder but also the breastfeeding stage. Christa makes clear how many problems she faced when she first started nursing her baby:

> CHRISTA: 'My baby came some weeks earlier than expected, but he was healthy and everything was OK. Of course I had to take all possible care that he ate enough and was growing. I wanted to breastfeed,

because that is best for the baby. Although I was inclined to eat less in order to lose extra weight after the birth, I also had to eat and to drink enough in order to be able to breastfeed. The responsibility for my baby was an important reason not to diet, but my idea that my stomach was still overweight strongly drew me towards going on a diet. I really had to struggle between my positive feelings for my baby and my negative view of my belly; fortunately my baby won.'

The fear about increased weight often disappears after a few months.

JOYCE: 'Since I stopped breastfeeding I have a stable weight. Seeing that my body was able to adapt to these fundamental processes of pregnancy and breastfeeding gave me a basic feeling of trust in my body. Now I am very happy that I survived that life-threatening anorexia nervosa. I was able to recover from my eating disorder, and even was able to give life to a beautiful son and feed him with my own body. Now I feel very proud of my body.'

Questionnaire about developing better social contacts

In this questionnaire, you can indicate whether you have improved your social relations.

You can answer 1=no, 2=a little, 3=somewhat, 4=yes, 5=very much

1.	I no longer feel isolated	1	2	3	4	5
2.	I participate in social activities	1	2	3	4	5
3.	I am able to initiate contacts with others	1	2	3	4	5
4.	I have some friends	1	2	3	4	5
5.	I have an intimate friend	1	2	3	4	5
6.	I have improved my relation with my parents	1	2	3	4	5
7.	I follow a course or study	1	2	3	4	5
8.	I do voluntary work	1	2	3	4	5
9.	I have a job	1	2	3	4	5

Other social improvements are:

10.	....	1	2	3	4	5
11.	....	1	2	3	4	5

Summary

This chapter was about reintegration after a period of severe social isolation during an eating disorder. To develop a feeling of trust in the therapeutic relation, a stable relationship is very crucial for patients, who often feel insecure in their relation with others. Recovered patients described how they learned to talk more openly about their emotions and inner thoughts and no longer hid them from others. They learned to participate in social activities and to develop new relations and friends. They developed the confidence to resume their school education and job or involved themselves in some voluntary work. This increased their social contacts and their self-esteem. For recovered patients, getting into an intimate relationship was very helpful. Although experiences with pregnancy and breastfeeding often produce ambivalent feelings, patients can learn to overcome their fear of weight increase and become proud of themselves and their body.

11

The Most Important Questions and Answers about Recovery

Introduction

In this chapter, you will find answers to the most important questions about recovery from eating disorders. When have eating disorder patients recovered? How many patients recover from their eating disorder? Why do not all patients recover? How can the recovery rate increase? Do all patients have a relapse? How long does it take to recover from an eating disorder? What are the important goals for treatment? Which treatments are most effective? What makes a good therapist? All these questions are answered in this chapter.

When have Eating Disorder Patients Recovered?

It is difficult to find a clear definition of recovery from an eating disorder in the literature (Berkman, Lohr, & Bulik, 2007; Couturier & Lock, 2006a; Kordy et al., 2002; Noordenbos, 2010; Rorty, Yager, & Rosotto, 1993). Jarman and Walsh (1999) found that the definitions used by therapists varied widely and that each definition gave different percentages of recovery. For a long time, the concept of recovery from an eating disorder covered no more than the improvement of eating habits and low weight (Windauer, Lennerts, Talbot, Touyz, & Beumont, 1993). This means that only the visible symptoms are reduced, but not the underlying factors (Bruch, 1978; Cogley & Keel, 2003). As long as the underlying factors have not improved, the risk of relapse

Recovery from Eating Disorders: A Guide for Clinicians and Their Clients,
First Edition. Greta Noordenbos.
© 2013 John Wiley & Sons, Ltd. Published 2013 by John Wiley & Sons, Ltd.

is quite high (Couturier & Lock, 2006b). Strober, Freeman, and Morrell (1997) evaluate the reduction of symptoms as only *partial recovery*.

For *full recovery*, Strober et al. (1997) conclude that it is necessary that all symptoms of anorexia and bulimia nervosa stay away for a period of several months. Moreover, patients should be able to maintain a normal weight and should no longer have binges and resort to compensating behaviour such as vomiting and using laxatives or slimming pills, as well as falling victim to excessive exercising and weight phobia. They should no longer worry about the amount of food intake and no longer check their weight frequently.

According to recovered eating disorder patients, full recovery implicates the following criteria: to eat healthy amounts of food and to maintain a healthy weight without being afraid of becoming overweight; to have a positive body attitude and increased self-esteem; to have better coping strategies; to regulate and express their emotions and to have better social contacts (Barran, Weltzin, & Kaye, 1995; Björk & Ahlström, 2008; Deter, 1992; Noordenbos & Seubring, 2006; Pettersen & Rosenvinge, 2002; Vanderlinden et al., 2007). It is also important to deal with *comorbidity*, such as alcohol abuse, depression, fear disorders, personality disorders and so on (Saccomani, Savoini, Cirrincione, & Ravera, 1989; Steinhausen, 2002).

How many Patients Recover from their Eating Disorder?

Steinhausen (1999, 2002) analysed the effects and outcomes of several studies on anorexia and bulimia nervosa and used the following measures for good, moderate and bad recovery.

In the case of *anorexia nervosa*, the outcome was evaluated as *good* when weight was within a range of 15% of the normal weight and menstruation was regular; the outcome was *moderate* when weight was lower than 15% of the normal weight and menstruation was irregular; the outcome was measured as *bad* when weight was lower than 85% of the normal weight and the patient did not menstruate, and also when the patient had developed bulimia nervosa. Steinhausen (2002) analysed 119 studies and found that 45% of the anorexia nervosa patients had recovered well, 35% had improved and 20% had a chronic eating disorder. Around 5% of the anorectic patients had died.

In case of recovery from *bulimia nervosa*, the outcome measures were based on the reduction of binging and purging behaviour. The outcome was evaluated as *good* when patients no longer had binges and purged; the outcome was seen as *moderate* when patients had reduced the number of binges and the frequency of purging behaviour; the outcome was considered as *bad* when bulimic patients continued to have binges followed by purging behaviour. Steinhausen (1999) found that 48% of bulimic patients had recovered well, 26% had improved and 26% had long-lasting bulimia nervosa.

In the study by Steinhausen, however, only two criteria for recovery were used, namely, weight recovery and menstruation for anorexia nervosa and reduction of binging and purging for bulimia nervosa. No psychological and social criteria were included in determining recovery from anorexia and bulimia nervosa. Many studies, however, show that limiting the outcome criteria to the most visible symptoms is not enough to measure full recovery (Noordenbos, 2011; Ratnasurya et al., 1991). According to Strober et al. (1997), these reduced criteria for recovery only reflect partial recovery. To ascertain full recovery, psychological and social criteria should also be taken into account.

Why do Not All Patients not Recover?

Research shows that eating disorder patients can recover quite well and that full recovery is possible for many patients. In general, 50% of anorexia and bulimia nervosa patients recover, 30% improve and 20% stay ill (Steinhausen, 1999, 2002). The percentage of recovered patients with bulimia nervosa is somewhat higher. Recently, the percentage of recovered patients has begun to increase, because of earlier diagnosis and better treatment (Elburg, 2007c). For adolescent eating disorders, recovery rates of 85% have been achieved (Nilsson & Hagglöff, 2006).

However, not all eating disorder patients recover (Keller, Herzog, Lavori, Bradborn, & Mahoney, 1992; Tierney & Fox, 2009). There have been only a few studies that have focused on patients who have not recovered even after many years (Noordenbos, Oldenhave, Muschter, & Terpstra, 2002). Factors that severely hamper recovery from eating disorders are a late diagnosis, patients' and doctors' delays, late and inadequate treatment focusing only on partial recovery such as food intake and weight increase without paying any attention to reducing the underlying factors, lack of aftercare and lack of relapse prevention. The longer patients have had an eating disorder, the more difficult it is for them to change their eating habits and deal with the physical, psychological and social consequences.

When treatment is directed exclusively at changing patients' eating habits and weight, the underlying factors remain. Thus, they will continue to have a negative body attitude and self-evaluation, will avoid negative emotions and will suffer from traumatic experiences, thereby increasing the risk of dropping out as well as relapse (Noordenbos et al., 2002). When the eating disorder becomes their main coping strategy for survival, it is very difficult for them to deal with it. As they do not learn to develop alternative coping strategies for their psychological, emotional and social problems, they run the risk of developing a long-lasting eating disorder. If treatment is inadequate and ineffective, patients lose all hope of improvement and recovery, affecting their trust in the treatment (Noordenbos et al., 2002).

Other reasons for a negative evaluation of their therapy might be that the relation with the therapist is not felt to be positive and helpful or that the therapy might be too short, hindering patients from making substantial progress. Moreover, patients who suffer from severe comorbidity, such as depression, obsessive compulsive disorder, personality disorder or a post-traumatic stress disorder, find it more difficult to recover from an eating disorder (Steinhausen, 1999, 2002). Lack of support from family members or strained family relationships is another factor which makes it difficult to overcome an eating disorder.

How can the Recovery Rate Increase?

What can be done to increase the number of patients who recover from an eating disorder? First of all, it is important to diagnose the eating disorder at an early stage. Parents, teachers, general practitioners and patients themselves have to become sensitive to the risk factors and first signs of an eating disorder. A second step is to find adequate and effective treatment as soon as the first signs of an eating disorder are noticed. In order to motivate patients for treatment, it is important that the treatment be focused not only on addressing food intake and weight issues but also on improving self-esteem and body attitude as well as emotion regulation and social coping strategies. To realize these goals, the treatment has to last long enough for patients to get accustomed to the new experiences. After the treatment, a long period of aftercare is necessary in order to reduce the risk of relapse. If patients have a relapse, it is important that they or their family members recognize the first signs at an early stage so that they receive support for their problems at the earliest (Berends, Elburg, & Meyel, 2010). In case of serious relapse, the patient should consult a therapist or visit a clinic for eating disorders so that she can continue her treatment.

Do All Patients have a Relapse?

Although most eating disorder patients remain vulnerable to checking their weight frequently and continuing with their diet, not all have a relapse after treatment. Having a relapse is closely related to the quality of treatment and the degree to which the most important criteria for recovery are realized. When treatment is directed only at partial recovery and merely focuses on reducing the most visible symptoms of eating habits and weight, the risk of a relapse is very high (Fennig, Fennig, & Roe, 2002; Kordy et al., 2002; Strober et al., 1997). Strober et al. (1997) showed that when treatment was directed only at recovery from eating habits and weight loss, the risk of relapse varied from 30% to 75% in the first year after treatment.

However, when the therapy has been directed at full recovery and the patient has learned to eat in a more healthy way, has developed a positive body attitude and more self-esteem, is able to accept and to express emotions and has developed better social coping strategies, the risk of relapse is much less and reduces to only 15% (Fennig et al., 2002; Strober et al., 1997). The more the treatment focuses on full recovery, the lower the risk of relapse.

Although full recovery takes more time than partial recovery, the effect is much more complete and lasting, and the risk of relapse is much less. After full recovery, most patients do not need further treatment. The total cost of treatment is less than in the case partial recovery followed by relapses and further treatment. Full recovery is important not only for patients and their families, but also for health insurance companies.

How long does it Take to Recover from an Eating Disorder?

Patients with a serious eating disorder cannot recover in a few weeks or months. The recovery process can take a minimum of six months or a year, depending on the duration and the severity of the eating disorders and the physical, psychological and social consequences, but often takes more time in order to stabilize full recovery and prevent a relapse (Clausen, 2004). For most eating disorder patients, the recovery process may take several years (Theander, 1985).

The earlier the eating disorder is diagnosed and treated, the shorter the duration of the treatment (Steinhausen, 1999, 2002). A major problem, however, is that in the first stage of their eating disorder most patients are not at all motivated to change their eating habits, because they experience their eating disorder as a *solution* for underlying problems. The question is how to motivate them to change their behaviour and to find effective treatment. However, even after they have been motivated to undergo treatment, they can lose their motivation if the therapy does not take into account their fundamental fears and underlying problems. Many patients lose their motivation if the therapy focuses only on food and weight and does not address their psychological, emotional and social problems. Recovery from an eating disorder is a complex process which should act not only at the physical level but should also take psychological, emotional and social factors into account.

Strober et al. (1997) and Fennig et al. (2002) have shown that improving eating habits and physical complaints takes around three to six months, but for psychological, emotional and social recovery, at least a year and a half is required. When family relationships are strained, it can take even more time to recover (Eckert, Halmi, Marchi, Grove, & Crosby, 1995; Fennig et al., 2002; Herzog, Rathner, & Vandereycken, 1992; Strober et al., 1997). All these studies show that without psychological recovery the risk of relapse is quite high, necessitating further treatment. If patients discontinue the therapy after only partial recovery, the risk of relapse is high, and recurrent treatments make the process of recovery quite long. Patients run the risk to losing trust in the treatment, and if the situation does not improve, they become convinced that they are not curable (Noordenbos et al., 2002).

What are the Important Goals for Treatment?

To achieve recovery from an eating disorder, it is not enough to focus the treatment on achieving a normal weight and eating habits (Hall & Orstoff, 1998). For full recovery, it is important that not only symptoms and conse- quences of an eating disorder disappear but also underlying factors, such as low self-esteem, negative body attitude, dysfunctional emotion regulation and lack of coping strategies. To realize full recovery, the following goals for treatment are important: improving patients' self-esteem and body attitude so that their self-worth is no longer related to their weight and eating hab- its and they no longer feel fat or have the urge to diet in an extreme way. Moreover, they should be able to eat healthy amounts of food and have a positive attitude to food. Improving emotion regulation is another impor- tant goal in the treatment of eating disorders, so that patients learn to accept and express their negative emotions and no longer try to avoid and suppress them. They have to become more assertive so that they no longer try to please others in order to be accepted or are afraid to be criticized or rejected. It is also important that they reduce their perfectionism and get rid of the fear of failure and learn to value themselves. To reduce their isolation, better social coping strategies have to be developed. These criteria for recovery can be translated into the following goals for treatment:

1. reducing the disturbed eating habits
2. reducing the physical, psychological and social consequences
3. developing a positive body image
4. developing self-esteem and a positive self-evaluation
5. recognizing, accepting and expressing emotions
6. developing social coping strategies and better social relations

Which Treatments are Most Effective?

Unfortunately, not all treatments for eating disorders are successful. As has become clear, treatments that focus only on normalizing eating habits and weight are not successful in realizing full recovery and often result in relapse

(Strober et al., 1997). Treatments that are directed at a broad spectrum of goals such as healthy food intake, physical recovery, a positive body image and more self-esteem, as well as better emotion regulation and social reintegration, are much more effective in realizing full recovery. Healing underlying problems and changing core beliefs of eating disorder patients is essential for full recovery (Jones, Harris, & Leung, 2005).

The most effective treatments for eating disorders are Cognitive Behaviour Therapy (CBT) (Agras & Apple, 1997; Fairburn, Cooper, & Shafran, 2003; Fairburn et al., 2008), Interpersonal Therapy (IPT) (Agras, Walsh, Fairburn, Wilson, & Kraemer, 2000), Body-Oriented Therapy and Multifamily Therapy (Asen, 2002; Colahan & Robinson, 2002; Dare & Eisler, 2000). Recently, therapies involving Acceptance and Commitment Therapy (ACT) (Hayes, Strosahl, & Wilson, 1999; Heffner & Eifert, 2004) and Mindfulness have also emerged as quite promising (Baer, 2003; Baer, Fischer, & Huss, 2005; Kristeller, Baer, & Wolever, 2006; Kristeller & Wolever, 2011). Many successful treatments use an eclectic approach in which different aspects of the most effective therapies are integrated. However, an important condition for a successful treatment is to share a good rapport with an experienced therapist.

What Makes a Good Therapist?

A positive relation with a therapist is very important for the success of the treatment (Agras et al., 2000). When patients do not have a good relationship with their therapist, they will not feel safe and may even lose motivation for the therapy and decide to drop out at an early stage of the treatment. De la Rie et al. (2006, 2008) did a study in which eating disorder patients were asked what they thought were the qualities of a good therapist. The following characteristics were mentioned as important (De la Rie & Libbers, 2004).

A good therapist:

- has specialized knowledge and experience of treating eating disorder patients;
- shows appreciation for the patient's problems;
- is able to view the situation from the client's perspective;
- takes the patient seriously;
- is able to listen to the patient;
- shows respect;
- gives clear information about the eating disorder and the treatment;
- has enough time for the patient;
- is able to put the patient at ease;

- dares to confront the patient;
- gives clear feedback;
- motivates the patient;
- provides insight into the characteristics and background of the eating disorder;
- regularly evaluates the treatment.

Many of the qualities for therapists which are evaluated as important by eating disorder patients are about the relation between the therapist and the patient, such as being able to understand the patient's perspectives and to take them seriously. Therefore, former eating disorder patients who have recovered quite well and have professionally specialized in the treatment of eating disorders are expected to have good qualities as therapists. They can also function as role models for patients who continue to struggle with their eating disorders as they will understand the problems that patients face better. However, it is still to be ascertained as to whether therapists who have recovered from an eating disorder have equal or even more success in the treatment of eating disorders.

Summary

In this chapter, answers have been provided to the most important questions concerning recovery from eating disorders. For full recovery, it is not only the symptoms of the eating disorder that have to be cured but also the underlying factors for the development of the eating disorder. The following criteria are important for full recovery: healthy eating habits, a healthy and stable weight, a positive body attitude, recovery from all kinds of physical consequences of the eating disorder, more self-esteem and better emotion regulation and social integration.

In general, 50% of anorexia nervosa patients recover, 30% improve and 20% remain ill. The percentage of recovered patients with bulimia nervosa is somewhat higher. Recently, the percentage of recovered patients has begun to increase, because of earlier diagnosis and better treatment. However, not all eating disorder patients recover. Factors that severely hamper recovery from eating disorders are a late diagnosis, patients' and doctors' delay, late and inadequate treatment focusing only on partial recovery such as food intake and weight increase without paying attention to reducing the underlying factors, lack of aftercare and lack of relapse prevention.

To increase the recovery rate, it is important to diagnose the eating disorder at an early stage and to find adequate and effective treatment at the earliest. The earlier the eating disorder is diagnosed and treated effectively, the shorter the duration of the treatment.

Depending on the duration and the severity of the eating disorder and the physical, psychological and social consequences, the recovery process can take a minimum of six months or a year, but often takes more time in order to stabilize full recovery and prevent relapse. Treatments directed at a broad spectrum of goals such as healthy food intake, physical recovery, a positive body image and more self-esteem, as well as better emotion regulation and social reintegration, are effective in realizing full recovery. In order to realize these goals, the treatment has to last long enough for patients to get accustomed to the new experiences. After the treatment, a long period of aftercare is necessary in order to reduce the risk of relapse.

12

Checklist for Full Recovery

Introduction

In this final chapter, questionnaires are presented by which you can check the most important aspects of recovery from an eating disorder: eating habits, body attitude, physical recovery, self-esteem, emotion regulation and social relations. When you fill out these questionnaires, you can see which aspects you have already improved upon and which aspects might need more attention. It may also be possible that you have realized some additional goals which are important for you but which are not mentioned in these questionnaires. You can add these criteria in the blank spaces provided. If you still have problems with some of the aspects mentioned in these checklists, you can discuss this with your therapist and try to find what treatment would be helpful.

A. Questionnaire about healthy eating habits

Do you meet the following criteria for healthy eating habits? Circle the right answer.

You can answer 1=no, 2=a little, 3=somewhat, 4=yes, 5=very well

A1.	My eating habit is healthy and regular	1	2	3	4	5
A2.	I eat three meals a day	1	2	3	4	5
A3.	Calorie intake is healthy and sufficient	1	2	3	4	5
A4.	I have no binges	1	2	3	4	5

Recovery from Eating Disorders: A Guide for Clinicians and Their Clients,
First Edition. Greta Noordenbos.
© 2013 John Wiley & Sons, Ltd. Published 2013 by John Wiley & Sons, Ltd.

A5.	I do not vomit after food intake	1	2	3	4	5
A6.	I do not use laxatives	1	2	3	4	5
A7.	I do not use diuretics	1	2	3	4	5
A8.	I do not use slimming pills	1	2	3	4	5
A9.	I do not do extreme exercising	1	2	3	4	5
A10.	I do not drink too much alcohol	1	2	3	4	5

Others aspects of improving my eating habits:

A11.	....	1	2	3	4	5
A12.	....	1	2	3	4	5
A13.	....	1	2	3	4	5

B. Questionnaire about a positive body attitude

Do you meet the following criteria for improving your body attitude? Circle the right answer.

You can answer 1=no, 2=a little, 3=somewhat, 4=yes, 5=very well

B1.	I do not feel too fat	1	2	3	4	5
B2.	I have a more positive body attitude	1	2	3	4	5
B3.	I can accept my appearance and figure	1	2	3	4	5
B4.	I do not feel the need to diet	1	2	3	4	5
B5.	I am not obsessed by my weight	1	2	3	4	5

Other aspects of improving your body attitude:

B6.	....	1	2	3	4	5
B7.	....	1	2	3	4	5
B8.	....	1	2	3	4	5

C. Questionnaire about physical recovery

Do you meet the following criteria for physical recovery? Circle the right answer.

You can answer 1=no, 2=a little, 3=somewhat, 4=yes, 5=very well

C1.	My weight is normal for my age and height	1	2	3	4	5
C2.	My weight has been stable for the past three months	1	2	3	4	5
C3.	I have monthly periods	1	2	3	4	5
C4.	My periods are regular	1	2	3	4	5
C5.	My body temperature is normal	1	2	3	4	5
C6.	My heart rate is normal	1	2	3	4	5

		1	2	3	4	5
C7.	My blood pressure is normal	1	2	3	4	5
C8.	I have no constipation	1	2	3	4	5
C9.	I have no bowel problems	1	2	3	4	5
C10.	I have no stomach problems	1	2	3	4	5
C11.	My skin is not dry	1	2	3	4	5
C12.	I have healthy teeth and gums	1	2	3	4	5
C13.	My sleeping pattern is normal	1	2	3	4	5
C14.	I do not feel very tired	1	2	3	4	5
C15.	I have enough energy	1	2	3	4	5

Other aspects of physical recovery:

C16.	....	1	2	3	4	5
C17.	....	1	2	3	4	5
C18.	....	1	2	3	4	5

D. Questionnaire about psychological recovery

Do you meet the following criteria for psychological recovery? Circle the right answer.

You can answer 1=no, 2=a little, 3=somewhat, 4=yes, 5=very well

D1.	I have enough self-esteem	1	2	3	4	5
D2.	My self-esteem is not related to my weight	1	2	3	4	5
D3.	I evaluate myself in a positive way	1	2	3	4	5
D4.	I do not criticize myself very often	1	2	3	4	5
D5.	I do not have negative thoughts about myself	1	2	3	4	5
D6.	I am not a perfectionist	1	2	3	4	5
D7.	I do not fear failure	1	2	3	4	5
D8.	I have a realistic image of myself	1	2	3	4	5
D9.	I can concentrate quite well	1	2	3	4	5
D10.	I can relax	1	2	3	4	5

Other aspects of psychological recovery:

D11.	....	1	2	3	4	5
D12.	....	1	2	3	4	5
D13.	....	1	2	3	4	5

E. Questionnaire about coping better with emotions

Do you meet the following criteria for coping with your emotions? Circle the right answer.

You can answer 1=no, 2=a little, 3=somewhat, 4=yes, 5=very well

E1.	I do not feel depressed	1	2	3	4	5
E2.	I am able to recognize my feelings and emotions	1	2	3	4	5
E3.	I am able to express negative emotions	1	2	3	4	5
E4.	I am able to express positive emotions	1	2	3	4	5
E5.	I do not do things just to please others	1	2	3	4	5
E6.	I do not depend on others' approval	1	2	3	4	5
E7.	I dare to express my own opinions	1	2	3	4	5
E8.	I am not afraid of having a different opinion	1	2	3	4	5
E9.	I can cope with stress in a healthy way	1	2	3	4	5

Other aspects of improving emotion regulation:

E10.	....	1	2	3	4	5
E11.	....	1	2	3	4	5

F. Questionnaire about better social relationships

Do you meet the following criteria for better social relationships? Circle the right answer.

You can answer 1=no, 2=a little, 3=somewhat, 4=yes, 5=very well

F1.	I do not feel isolated	1	2	3	4	5
F2.	I participate in social events and activities	1	2	3	4	5
F3.	I am able to initiate contact with others	1	2	3	4	5
F4.	I have some good friends	1	2	3	4	5
F5.	I dare to talk about personal experiences	1	2	3	4	5
F6.	The contact with my parents is good enough	1	2	3	4	5
F7.	I do some voluntary work	1	2	3	4	5
F8.	I have enrolled in a course or study programme	1	2	3	4	5
F9.	I have a job	1	2	3	4	5

Other social goals which are important for me:

F10.	....	1	2	3	4	5
F11.	....	1	2	3	4	5

If you have answered some aspects with 1, 2 or 3, you can ask your therapist to help you to realize these criteria for recovery. If you have answered some aspects with a 4 or 5, you have improved a lot!

Conclusion

When you have filled out these checklists you have a clear idea how well you have improved or recovered from the symptoms and consequences of your eating disorder. This checklist for recovery will also make clear which problems you still have. For example, you may still have a negative attitude towards your body, or lack self esteem, or suffer from several physical consequences, or have emotional and social problems. In that case this checklist can be helpful to make clear which aspects might be improved in your treatment. It is important that you discuss your answers with your therapist in order to explore what might be a useful therapy for you to realize these goals.

In this book you have read how many former patients were able to recover and their experiences may motivate you to make your own steps on the way to recovery. Good luck!

References

American Psychiatric Association (2000). *DSM-IV: Diagnostic and statistical manual of mental disorders* (4th ed., text revision). Washington, DC: American Psychiatric Association.

Agras, W.S., & Apple, R.F. (1997). *Overcoming eating disorders. A cognitive-behavioral treatment for bulimia nervosa and binge eating disorder.* Therapist guide. San Antonio: The Psychological Corporation, Hartcourt Brace & Company.

Agras, W.S., Walsh, B.T., Fairburn, C.G., Wilson, G.T., & Kraemer, H.C. (2000). A multicenter comparison of cognitive-behavioral therapy and interpersonal psychotherapy for bulimia nervosa. *Archives of General Psychiatry, 57*, 459–466.

Asen, E. (2002). Multifamily therapy: An overview. *Journal of Family Therapy, 24*, 3–16.

Baer, R.A. (2003). Mindfulness training as a clinical intervention: A conceptual and empirical review. *Clinical Psychology: Science and Practice, 10*, 125–143.

Baer, R.A., Fischer, S., & Huss, D.B. (2005). Mindfulness-based cognitive therapy applied to binge eating: A case study. *Cognitive and Behavioral Practice, 12*, 351–358.

Barran, S.A., Weltzin, T.E., & Kaye, W.H. (1995). Low discharge weight and out-come in anorexia nervosa. *American Journal of Psychiatry, 152*, 1070–1072.

Beales, D.L., & Dolton, R. (2000). Eating disordered patients: Personality, alexithymia, and implications for primary care. *British Journal of General Practice, 50*, 21–26.

Berends, T., Elburg, A. A., van, & Meyel, B. van. (2010). *Guideline for relapse prevention of anorexia nervosa.* Van Gorcum, Assen (in Dutch).

Berkman, N.D., Lohr, K.N., & Bulik, C.M. (2007). Outcomes of eating disorders: A systematic review of the literature. *International Journal of Eating Disorders, 40*, 293–309.

Recovery from Eating Disorders: A Guide for Clinicians and Their Clients,
First Edition. Greta Noordenbos.
© 2013 John Wiley & Sons, Ltd. Published 2013 by John Wiley & Sons, Ltd.

Björk, T., & Ahlström, G. (2008). The patients' perception on having recovered from an eating disorder. *Health Care for Women International, 29*, 926–944.

Bloks, H., & Spaans, J. (2008). Recognition and diagnostic. In: W. Vandereycken, & G. Noordenbos (Eds.), *Handbook eating disorders* (pp. 87–118). Utrecht: De Tijdstroom (in Dutch).

Bruch, H. (1978). *The golden cage: The enigma of anorexia nervosa.* Cambridge, MA: Harvard University Press.

Cervera, S., Lahortiga, F., Martinez-Gonzalez, M.A., Gual, P., Irala-Estevez, J. de., & Alfonso, Y. (2003). Neuroticism and low self-esteem as risk factors of incident eating disorders in a prospective cohort study. *International Journal of Eating Disorders, 33*, 271–280.

Claude-Pierre, P. (1997). *The secret language of eating disorders.* Random House, Inc, New York.

Clausen, L. (2004). Time course of symptom remission in eating disorders. *International Journal of Eating Disorders, 36*, 296–306.

Cogley, C.B., & Keel, P.K. (2003). Requiring remission of undue influence of weight and shape on self-evaluation in the definition of recovery from bulimia nervosa. *International Journal of Eating Disorders, 34*, 200–210.

Colahan, M., & Robinson, P.H. (2002). Multi-family groups in the treatment of young adults with eating disorders. *Journal of Family Therapy, 24*, 17–30.

Couturier, J., & Lock, J. (2006a). What is recovery in adolescent anorexia nervosa? *International Journal of Eating Disorders, 39*, 550–555.

Couturier, J., & Lock, J. (2006b). What is remission in adolescent anorexia nervosa? A review of various conceptualizations and quantitative analysis. *International Journal of Eating Disorders, 39*, 175–183.

Dare, C., & Eisler, I. (2000). A multi-family group day treatment programme for adolescent eating disorder. *European Eating Disorders Review, 8*, 4–18.

Deter, H.C. (1992). The anorexia nervosa symptom score: A multidimensional tool for evaluating the course of anorexia nervosa. In W. Herzog, H.C. Deter, & W. Vandereycken (Eds.), *The course of eating disorders. Long term follow up studies of anorexia and bulimia nervosa* (pp. 40–52). London: Springer-Verlag.

Dolhanty, J., & Greenberg, L.S. (2009). Emotion-focused therapy in a case of anorexia nervosa. *Clinical Psychology & Psychotherapy, 16*, 366–382.

Eckert, E.D., Halmi, K.A., Marchi, P., Grove, W., & Crosby, R. (1995). Ten year follow-up of anorexia nervosa. Clinical course and outcome. *Psychological Medicine, 25*, 143–156.

Elburg, A.A. van. (2007a). *Psychoneuroendocrinological aspects of anorexia nervosa: predictors of recovery.* Thesis (pp. 131–148). Enschede: Gildeprint Drukkerijen BV.

Elburg, A.A. van. (2007b). Changes in mood states during recovery from anorexia nervosa. In A.A. van Elburg (Ed.), *Psychoneuroendocrinological aspects of anorexia nervosa: predictors of recovery.* Thesis (pp. 131–148). Enschede: Gildeprint Drukkerijen BV.

Elburg, A.A. van. (2007c). Outcome of anorexia nervosa: Results of a 5 year follow-up study. In A.A. van Elburg (Ed.), *Psychoneuroendocrinological aspects of anorexia nervosa: Predictors of recovery.* Thesis (pp. 149–172). Enschede: Gildeprint Drukkerijen BV.

Erikson, E.H. (1968). *Identity, youth and crisis*. W. W. Norton, New York.

Fairburn, C.G., Cooper, Z., & Shafran. (2003). Cognitive behaviour therapy for eating disorders: A 'transdiagnostic' theory and treatment. *Behaviour Research and Therapy, 41*, 509–528.

Fairburn, C.G., Cooper, Z., Shafran, R., Hawker, D.M., Murphy, R., & Straebler, S. (2008). Enhanced cognitive behaviour therapy for eating disorders: The core protocol. In C.G. Fairburn (Ed.), *Cognitive behaviour therapy for eating disorders*. New York: Guilford.

Fairburn, C.G., Welch, S.I., Doll, H.A., Davies, B.A., & O'Connor, M.E. (1997). Risk factors for bulimia nervosa: A community-based case-control study. *Archives of General Psychiatry, 54*, 509–517.

Fennig, S., Fennig, G., & Roe, D. (2002). Physical recovery in anorexia nervosa: Is this the sole purpose of a child and adolescent medical psychiatric unit? *General Hospital Psychiatry, 24*, 87–92.

Fodor, V. (1997). *Desperately seeking self. An inner guidebook for people with eating disorders*. Carlsbad: Gürze Books.

Fox, J.R.E. (2009). Eating disorders and emotions. *Clinical Psychology and Psychotherapy, 16*, 237–239.

Gilbert, P. (2010). *Compassion focused therapy*. London: Routledge, Taylor & Francis Group.

Hall, L., & Orstoff, M. (1998). *Anorexia nervosa: A guide to recovery*. Gürze Books, Carlsbad, CA.

Hayes, S.C., Strosahl, K.D., & Wilson, K.G. (1999). *Acceptance and commitment therapy*. New York: Guilford Press.

Heffner, M., & Eifert, G.H. (2004). *The Anorexia workbook. How to accept yourself, heal your suffering, and reclaim your life*. Oakland: New Harbinger publications, Inc.

Herzog, W., Rathner, G., & Vandereycken, W. (1992). Long-term course of Anorexia nervosa: A review of the literature. In D.B. Herzog, H.-C., Deter, & W. Vandereycken (Eds.), *The course of eating disorders* (pp. 15–39). Berlin: Springer-Verlag.

Jacobi, C., de Zwaan, M., Hayward, C., Kraemer, H.C., & Agras, W.S. (2004). Coming to terms with risk factors for eating disorders: Application of risk factors terminology and suggestions for a general taxonomy. *Psychological Bulletin, 130*, 19–65.

Jantz, G.L., & Mc Murray, A. (2002). *Hope and healing for eating disorders. A new approach to treating anorexia, bulimia and overeating*. Colorado: Waterbrook Press.

Jarman, M., & Walsh, S. (1999). Evaluating recovery from anorexia nervosa and bulimia nervosa: Integrating lessons learned from research and clinical practice. *Clinical Psychological Review, 19*, 773–788.

Jimerson, D.C., Wolfe, B.E., Franko, D.L., Colvino, N.A., & Sifneos, P.E. (1994). Alexithymia ratings in bulimia: Clinical correlates. *Psychosomatic Medicine, 56*, 90–93.

Jones, C., Harris, G., & Leung, N. (2005). Core beliefs and eating disorders recovery. *European Eating Disorders Review, 13*, 237–244.

Keel, P.M. (2005). *Eating disorders*. New Jersey: Pearson. Prentice Hall.

Keel, P.K., Mitchell, J.E., Davis, T.L., Fieselman, S., & Crow, S.J. (2000). Impact of definitions on the description and prediction of bulimia nervosa outcome. *International Journal of Eating Disorders, 28*, 377–386.

Keller, M.B., Herzog, D.B., Lavori, P.W., Bradborn, I.S., & Mahoney, E.M. (1992). The naturalistic history of bulimia nervosa: Extraordinary high rates of chronicity, relapse, recurrence, and psychosocial morbidity. *International Journal of Eating Disorders, 12*, 1–9.

Kordy, H., Kramer, B., Palmer, B., Papezova, H., Pellet, J., & Richard, M., et al. (2002). Remission, recovery, relapse, and recurrence in eating disorders: Conceptualization and illustration of a validation strategy. *Journal of Clinical Psychology, 58*, 833–846.

Kortink, J. (2008). *Breaking the spell of binge-eating. A road to balance in your life*. Chicago: Academy Chicago Publishers.

Kristeller, J.L., Baer, R., & Wolever, R.Q. (2006). Mindfulness based approaches to eating disorders. In R. Baer (Ed.), *Mindfulness and acceptance-based interventions: Conceptualization, application, and empirical support*. San Diego, CA: Elsevier.

Kristeller, J.L., & Wolever, R.Q. (2011). Mindfulness-based awareness training for treating binge eating disorders: The conceptual foundation. *Eating Disorders: The Journal of Treatment and Prevention, 19*, 49–61.

Levenkrohn, S. (1979). *The best little girl in the world*. Chicago: Temporary Books.

Levine, M.P., & Smolak, L. (1998). The mass media and disordered eating: Implications for primary prevention. In W. Vandereycken, & G. Noordenbos (Eds.), *Prevention of eating disorders* (pp. 23–56). London: Athlone Press.

MacLeod, S. (1981). *The art of starvation. One girl's journey through adolescence and anorexia—A story of survival*. London: Virago Limited.

Miller, A. (1981). *Das Drama des begabten Kindes und die Suche nach dem wahren Selbst: Eine UM-und Fortschreibung*. In Dutch *Het drama van het begaafde kind*. Een studie over het narcisme. Bussum: Het Wereldvenster.

National Institute for Clinical Excellence (NICE, 2004). Eating Disorders – core interventions in the treatment and management of anorexia nervosa, bulimia nervosa, related eating disorders. NICE Clinical Guidelines No. 9. London: National Institute for Clinical Excellence.

Neff, K.D. (2003). Self compassion: An alternative conceptualization of a healthy attitude toward oneself. *Self and Identity, 2*, 85–102.

Neff, K.D. (2011). *Self-compassion*. New York: Harper Collins.

Nilsson, K., &. Hägglöff, B. (2006). Patients perspectives of recovery in adolescent onset Anorexia nervosa. *Eating Disorders: The Journal of Treatment and Prevention, 14*, 305–311.

Noordenbos, G. (2007). *Guide to recover from an Eating Disorder*. Utrecht, De Tijdstroom (In Dutch: Gids voor herstel van eetstoornissen).

Noordenbos, G. (2010). When have eating disorder patients recovered and what do the DSM-IV criteria tell about recovery? *Eating Disorders: The Journal of Treatment and Prevention, 19*, 234–245.

Noordenbos, G. (2011). Which criteria for recovery are relevant according to eating disorder patients and therapists? *Eating Disorders: The Journal of Treatment and Prevention, 19*, 441–451.

Noordenbos, G., Boesenach, K., Moerman, N., & Trommelen. (2012). *Hearing negative voices. Experiences of eating disorder patients*. (Thesis) Leiden, Leiden University.

Noordenbos, G., Oldenhave, A., Muschter. J., & Terpstra, N. (2002). Characteristics and treatment of patients with chronic eating disorders. *Eating Disorders: The Journal of Treatment and Prevention, 10*, 5–29.

Noordenbos, G., & Seubring, A. (2006). Criteria for recovery from eating disorders according to patients and therapists. *Eating Disorders: The Journal of Treatment and Prevention, 14*, 41–54.

Nottelman, M., & Thijsen, J. (2011). *Struggle. Mother and daughter in combat with anorexia*. Amsterdam: Van Gennep (in Dutch: Tweestrijd).

Pettersen, G., & Rosenvinge, J. H. (2002). Improvement and recovery from eating disorders: A patient perspective. *Eating Disorders: The Journal of Treatment and Prevention, 10*, 61–71.

Pinhas, L., Toner, B.A., Garfinkel, P.E., & Stuckless, N. (1999). Effects of the ideal of female beauty on mood and body satisfaction. *International Journal of Eating Disorders, 25*, 223–226.

Piran, N. (1999). The reduction of preoccupation with body weight and shape in schools: A feminist approach. In: N. Piran, M.P.Levine, & C. Steiner-Adair, (Eds.), *Preventing eating disorders. A handbook of interventions and special challenges* (pp. 148–162). Philadelphia: Brunner-Mazel.

Ratnasurya, R.H., Eisler, I., & Szmukler, G.I. (1991). Anorexia nervosa: Outcome and prognostic factors after 20 years. *British Journal of Psychiatry, 158*, 465–502.

Reindl, S.M. (2001). *Sensing the self. Women's recovery from bulimia*. London: Harvard University Press.

Rie, S. de la, & Libbers, L. (2004). *Take me serious. Guide for the treatment of eating disorders*. Amsterdam, SWP (in Dutch: Zie mij voor vol aan).

Rie, S. de la, Noordenbos, G., & Furth, E. van. (2006). Evaluation the treatment of eating disorders from the patients' perspective. *International Journal of Eating Disorders, 39*, 667–676.

Rie, S. de la, Noordenbos, G., & Furth, E. van. (2008). The quality of treatment of eating disorders: A comparison of the therapists' and the patients' perspective. *International Journal of Eating Disorders, 41*, 307–317.

Rorty, M., Yager, J., Buckwalter, J.G., & Rossotto, E. (1999). Social support, social adjustment, and recovery status in bulimia nervosa. *International Journal of Eating Disorders, 26*, 1–2.

Rorty, M., Yager, J., & Rosotto, E. (1993). Why and how do women recover from bulimia nervosa. The subjective appraisals of forty women recovered for a year or more. *International Journal of Eating Disorders, 14*, 249–160.

Saccomani, L., Savoini, M., Cirrincione, M., & Ravera, G. (1989). Long term outcome of children and adolescents with anorexia nervosa: Study of comorbidity. *Journal of Psychosomatic Research, 44*, 565–571.

Spaans, J., & Bloks, H. (2008). Motivation for change. In: W. Vandereycken, & G. Noordenbos (Eds.), *Handbook eating disorders* (pp. 119–154). Utrecht: De Tijdstroom (in Dutch).

Speranza, M., Loas, G., Wallier, J., & Corcos, M. (2007). Predictive value of alexithymia in patients with eating disorders: A 3-year prospective study. *Journal of Psychosomatic Research, 63*, 365–371.

Steinhausen, H.-C. (1999). Eating disorders. In H.-C. Steinhausen & F.C. Verhulst (Eds.), *Risks and outcomes in developmental psychopathology* (pp. 210–230). Oxford: Oxford University Press.

Steinhausen, H.-C. (2002). The outcome of anorexia nervosa in the 20th century. *American Journal of Psychiatry, 159*, 284–1293.

Sterk, F., & Swaen, S. (2006). *Positive selfmotivation.* Utrecht: Antwerpen, Lifetime, Kosmos–Z&K Uitgevers.

Stice, E. (2002). Risk and maintenance factors for eating pathology; a meta-analytic review. *Psychological Bulletin, 128*, 825–848.

Striegel-Moore, R.H., & Bulik, C.M. (2007). Risk factors for eating disorders. *American Psychologist, 62*, 181–198.

Strober, M., Freeman, R., & Morrell, W. (1997). The long term course of severe anorexia nervosa, in adolescents: Survival of recovery, relapse & outcome predictors over 10–15 years in a prospective study. *International Journal of Eating Disorders, 25*, 135–142.

Tenwolde, A.A.M. (2000). *From thin to fat. Psychosocial and biological aspects of anorexia nervosa, boulimia nervosa and obesitas.* Houten/Diegem: Bohn Stafleu Van Loghum (in Dutch Van dun tot dik).

Theander, S. (1985). Outcome and prognosis in anorexia nervosa and bulimia: Some results of previous investigations, compared with those of a Swedish long-term study. *Journal of Psychiatric Research, 19*, 493–508.

Tierney, S., & Fox, J.R.E. (2009). Chronic anorexia nervosa: A delphi study to explore practitioners' views. *International Journal of Disorders, 42*, 62–67.

Tierney, S., & Fox, J.R.E. (2010). Living with the 'anorexic voice': A thematic analysis. *Psychology and Psychotherapy: Theory, Research and Practice, 83*, 243–254.

Vandereycken, W., & Deth, R. van. (1994). *From fasting saints to anorexic girls. The history of self-starvation.* London: The Athlone Press.

Vanderlinden, J., Buis, H., Pieters, G., & Probst, M. (2007). Which elements in the treatment are 'necessary' ingredients in the recovery process. A comparison between patient's and therapist's view. *European Eating Disorders Review, 15*, 357–365.

Weezel, N. van. (2006). *Anorectic Years.* Amsterdam, Archipel (in Dutch: Magere jaren).

Windauer, U., Lennerts, W., Talbot, P., Touyz, S.W., & Beumont, P.J. (1993). How well are 'cured' anorexia nervosa patients? An investigation of 16 weight recovered anorexic patients. *British Journal of Psychiatry, 163*, 195–200.

Zonnevijlle-Bender, M.J.S., van Goozen, S.H.M., Cohen-Kettenis, P.T., van Elberg, A., & van Engeland, H. (2004). Emotional functioning in adolescent anorexia nervosa patients: A controlled study. *European Child & Adolescent Psychiatry, 13*, 28–34.

Index

Date Due

FEB 1 7 2015			
MAR 1 1 2015			
APR 0 1 2015			